Losing,

Leaving,

&

Letting

Go

SURVIVING THE
CHANGE POINTS
OF LIFE

by *Marceal Clark*

Losing, Leaving, and Letting Go
Surviving the Change Points of Life
by Marceal Clark

© 1994, Word Aflame Press
Hazelwood, MO 63042-2299

Cover Design by Tim Agnew

All Scripture quotations in this book are from the King James Version of the Bible unless otherwise identified.

Printed in United States of America

Printed by

Library of Congress Cataloging-in-Publication Data
Clark, Marceal.
     Losing, leaving, and letting go : surviving the change points of
     life / by Marceal Clark.
          p. cm.
     ISBN 1-56722-022-3   :
          1. Grief—Religious aspects—Christianity. 2. Consolation.
     3. Life change events—Religious aspects—Christianity. 4. Clark.,
     Marceal. I. Title.
     BV4509.5.C52 1944
     248.8′6—dc20   94-6853
                                                              CIP

TO
KEITH

*whose love of life taught me how to live;
whose antics with Prissy, Missy, and Skippy
taught me how to laugh; and whose love for me
taught me to hear the music again.*

Contents

PART I

Understanding Pain

Change 1 Point!

"**M**rs. Camp," the doctor's quiet voice intruded into my confused thoughts. It was about twenty minutes before 4:00 AM, June 2, 1986, and the doctor's voice was insistent.

"Mrs. Camp, you must make the decision of whether or not to have the life support system unhooked from your husband. Technically, he's already dead. There's no brain wave at all. Mrs. Camp, do you hear me?"

Yes, I hear you, Doctor, my thoughts were silently screaming. But I'm not God! How can I decide when it's time for a human life to end? Only God should have that power.

I had been sitting dazed and numbed in the same spot in the little hospital chapel the nurses had led me to over eight hours before.

How can he be "technically dead"? Please, God, he can't be dead! Why, less than forty-eight hours ago we had a family fun time with the kids—hamburgers—homemade ice cream. Please, God, no!

The team of doctors who had worked all night frantically trying to save my husband's life had given me no hope. "A ruptured abdominal aneurysm is almost always fatal," I was told. No hope. No hope.

I heard the low sobs of my three children and felt the grip of my pastor's hand as the doctor insisted upon my answer. Then I heard the quiet voice of my pastor saying, "Doctor, please give us a few moments to pray; then she will give you an answer."

My church family and friends had kept vigil with me all night at the hospital, and as they gathered once again around me and my children to pray, I felt God's love and concern for His hurting and confused children.

Listening to my pastor's voice as he prayed, my mind shifted to the events of the night before.

In excruciating pain, Cecil slumped onto the front seat of the car as it sprouted wings, and we flew to the hospital. As the nurses were hooking him up to an IV, he lapsed into unconsciousness. The artery had ruptured, they told me later.

"Honey, what's wrong?" I felt his forehead. It was cold and clammy. I began to cry as the nurses hurried me out of the room, knowing in my heart that this was the last time I would see my husband alive.

In our thirty-eight years of marriage, we had survived many hospital stays together—heart attacks, open-heart surgery—but this time it was different. This time the icy fingers of death were reaching out to take him.

Now, at the end of our eight-hour vigil, the doctor was insisting upon my answer. But I refused to play God!

At that moment, sensing my thoughts, my pastor gripped my hand again, saying quietly, "Just hold on. God will not require you to make that decision."

At 3:56 AM the doctor came in again. The look in his eyes spoke the words before he quietly said, "Mrs. Camp, the decision is out of your hands. The Almighty reached down and stopped the heartbeat."

• *Healing of the Memory* •

Who among us does not need a cleansing or a healing of memories?

What of the shattered dreams, and what of the regrets?

What of those unhealed inner scars we try to hide from everyone?

We need to admit, first, that they are there. We need the Lord to reopen the closed wound, to clean out the hidden infection, and to begin the process whereby the terrible hurts of our lives heal from the inside out. When we lay ourselves bare before Him, He will take the scalpel of His Spirit and begin the catharsis that cleanses the memory. Only the Lord can heal inner conflicts.

A physical wound limits what the body can do, but an emotional wound limits what the spirit can do. Wounded from hurts of life, we keep others at arm's length. Afraid to let anyone get too close, we shield ourselves from further hurts.

Thus isolated from others, we harbor and replay old hurts, thereby distorting our decisions and contributing to stress. Through distorted decisions, our self-worth is damaged, and those unhealed inner scars reach from the past into the present.

What of those memories? What of the regrets and inner scars?

We must confront and conquer those buried feelings,

for they will not only reach from the past and pursue us into the present but also chase us into the future. We cannot change the past, but with the Lord's help, we can change its hold on us.

Shattered dreams, disappointment, frustration, confusion: all play their part in unhealed memories. Loneliness, stress, depression, resentment, anger—these surface and need the scalpel of God's Spirit.

Difficult times come to us all. Our reaction to these change points of life will determine whether we will have healed or unhealed memories, acceptance or regret, an open wound or a healed scar.

I have been through much that I do not understand. God does not ask me to understand it but to accept it. He says, "What I do thou knowest not now; but thou shalt know hereafter" (John 13:7).

Surviving the Change Points

When I speak of surviving the change points of life, I do not suggest a philosophy of grit your teeth and bear it or get through the days as best you can. That approach is emotionally draining and eventually destroys the will to go on.

As a Christian, when I speak of survival, I refer to seeking out and choosing God's best ways for healthy survival, both emotionally and spiritually. The grit-your-teeth-and-bear-it syndrome is man's trying to survive without God. By contrast, God enables us to survive by using seeming defeats, turning them around, and making them into victories.

I read a news story recently about five skiers who got lost on the back slopes in Colorado in a blinding snowstorm. Presumed dead, they were all found alive five days later, much to the amazement of the search party.

In the interview, a news reporter asked, "How did you manage to survive?"

A skier replied that survival hinges on two things:

1. *You must stay hydrated.*
2. *You must stay warm.*

It was interesting to me that the primary survival tactics were not:

1. *Don't panic.*
2. *Stay calm.*

The skier knew that even if he did not panic and even if he remained calm, the bottom line of his survival depended upon his staying hydrated and staying warm.

In our survival of the change points of life, those basic survival skills also apply to us. The "living water" of God's Spirit will keep us alive. Jesus has promised never to forsake us. We have the means to stay hydrated and to stay warm.

We can be survivors!

• *Seasons of Life* •

What skills are built into humans to help them survive difficult times? Why do some people cope while others do not? Why do some resist even the normal phases of life?

One phase of life ends and another begins. Sometimes change is so gradual that we do not notice life's changing scenes.

For instance, I know a couple in their late thirties who attend church in another city. One day the wife said to me somewhat sheepishly, "Our pastor called all the young married couples to the front of the church. While we were trying to exit our pew, stumbling over feet and murmuring 'Excuse me,' he qualified his statement—all those under the age of thirty. Red-faced, humiliated, we quietly sat down."

Indeed, we are out of one phase of life and into another without being conscious of it. Time and change wait for no one.

A friend of mine went to the eye doctor recently for a routine exam and was told she needed bifocals. To add insult to injury, the doctor said, "You realize, of course, that you are in the phase of life when it's normal to need bifocals."

Complaining to me, my friend confessed that she had not known she was in that "phase of life." It crept up unawares. She further summed it up by saying, "The young adult who walked into the doctor's office walked out a middle-aged wreck!"

Likewise, time and change happen to us all. Do we learn from them, or do we try to hold on to the past?

Who among us has not seen a pathetic older woman trying desperately to cling to youth? Striving to recapture youth, she succeeds only in accentuating age.

Do we resist change, or can we flow with the change points of life? Assuredly, those who resist change will live out their lives being miserable and often blaming God.

Unquestionably, we live in a changing world where change is inevitable. This is the way the God of the universe planned it. He planned the changing seasons of nature, and He also planned the seasons of life.

In the natural world, the Lord has the reins of the wind in His hand. Rains and droughts are at His command. Storms yield and bow to His voice. He commands the wind to blow this way or that way, and it obeys. He commands the rains to pour here or there, and they obey. Clouds cannot so much as gather unless He allows them.

Likewise, He commands or allows the winds and storms of life. Assuredly, everything in life is in His control. Some things that we do not understand are the foundation or springboard for what He has planned for our life.

King Solomon said, "To every thing there is a season, and a time to every purpose under the heaven: a time to be born, and a time to die; . . . a time to weep, and a time to laugh; a time to mourn, and a time to dance; . . . a time to get, and a time to lose" (Ecclesiastes 3:1-6). This book focuses on the words—"a time to lose"—losing and leaving and letting go.

In the natural seasons, we associate certain types of weather with certain seasons. We expect it to be cold in the winter and hot in the summer. It is the little surprises, however, that spice up the season.

Unusually warm, sunshiny days sandwiched in the middle of a subfreezing winter cause us to drag out the gardening tools and seed catalogs. Shedding sweaters and coats, we happily dig up flower beds, content in doing the same task we considered drudgery in the summertime.

What makes the difference?

In the summer, it is the normal thing to dig in flower beds, but in the dead of winter, it is a welcome change, and we enjoy it.

Such is also true in the seasons of life. We grow from childhood through "teenhood" and into adulthood and finally reach "oldhood." Through those intervening years, we witness many changes. We get married, move to new neighborhoods, change jobs, have children. Our children grow up and leave the nest; our parents grow old.

Some changes we witness are good and give us pleasure, much like the pleasure of the unusually balmy day in the dead of winter. We smile and are able to flow with the change, enjoying it immensely. We fall in love, get a raise on the job, move into a beautiful new home, take a fabulous vacation. These are definite change points of life that require a change in our lifestyle, but most of us can happily cope with these types of change points.

It is when changes make us sad that we need to analyze our feelings, understand why we react as we do, and learn the coping skills necessary to survive.

• *Survival Requires Absolute Trust in Our Heavenly Father* •

In the course of childhood, many changes take place— our bodies change, our minds change. But if we had a happy childhood, we were secure in the knowledge that our parents had everything under control.

As a child growing up in West Texas during the oil boom days, I remember that life changed almost daily because of Dad's job. Dad was a driller with Magnolia Oil Company and constantly had to move from one well to the next. Consequently, we moved from town to town, school to school. It was not uncommon for my brother, Travis, and me to attend three or four different schools within the school year. I was forced constantly to change friends, change homes, and change schools.

Nevertheless, looking back at those growing-up years, all I can see is a happy, carefree youngster, content with her world.

Why?

I am sure it is because I had so much confidence in my

parents. Even as a little girl, I remember knowing the changes were necessary in order for Dad to keep his job. I knew my dad so well that I was convinced he would not inflict something on me that was harmful. I had absolute trust in him.

As I have gotten older, I have often thought about Dad. Why should he as a young man, and even after he got older, work such long, hard hours, seemingly untiring? Why should he cheerfully and consistently do such strenuous labor?

Then the answer came. It was so that by his example I might learn that life is not meaningful or fulfilling without sincere labor; that we have the privilege of honest work, the privilege to dream and to fail, and the privilege to pick ourselves up and to dream again.

Another thought I have had about Dad is this: as he neared retirement age, why did God allow him to lose nearly all his worldly possessions and almost his life in just a few fleeting moments of time—in a combination of wind and fire? Why?

Then the answer came. It was so that when my own world collapsed around me he would have the wisdom to say, "Pick up the pieces of your life and go forward."

I am thankful for Dad's exemplary life. I have absolute trust in him.

Similarly, if we have absolute trust in our heavenly Father, when changes occur in our lives, we will be secure in the knowledge that He will see us safely through them. When we have absolute trust in His character, we know that there is a plan and a purpose for each day in our journey of life.

Speaking of the journey of life, I remember as a youngster

growing up in the '30s and '40s the journey our family made each summer to my grandparents' farm. This pilgrimage was well over six hundred miles since they lived far away across the vast expanse of the state of Texas and into Louisiana. To my brother, Travis, and me this journey was the highlight of our year.

Back then, there were no superhighways. The main highway we traveled from our home on the Texas–New Mexico border to Grandmother's house in Louisiana was Highway 80, a narrow, two-lane road with many signal lights, stop signs, and detours.

I especially remember the detours.

With no warning, we would suddenly be routed onto scary, winding, bumpy trails with dangerous potholes and obstacles. But with Dad behind the wheel and Mother by his side faithfully guiding him via the highway signs and road map, we happily chugged along in our 1940 model Ford V-8. We were oblivious to the inconvenience of the journey because we were anticipating the end of the journey at Grandmother's house.

It has been said that the Christian is just a pilgrim on this earth journeying toward that city "whose builder and maker is God" (Hebrews 11:10). To be sure, we do not always travel on a superhighway.

In fact, the road to glory takes many turns, and detours are prevalent. Sometimes with no warning we find that we must leave the highway of comfort and ease where everything is running smoothly. We may have a good job and our health may be good, but then life forces us to detour onto that scary, unknown road of tragedy when loved ones are suddenly taken from us, when our health fails, or when finances vanish away.

Part of the excitement of the journey to Grandmother's house was spending the night in a tourist court (as motels were called back then). There were not many tourists in those days, and the tourist courts were not the clean, fashionable places we have come to expect the modern motel to be.

On the contrary, sometimes there were bugs, and sometimes there was dirt (even filth). It was part of the ritual of the journey for Mother to meticulously inspect our rooms for cleanliness before Dad would sign for them. Some of them were so terrible she would not dare let him sign, and we would travel down the road to the next tourist court, where the ritual would begin again. This was exciting to my brother and me as we followed Mother around those tiny rooms stalking bugs and dirt!

Likewise, as we anticipate the fun that life offers, we must constantly be on guard to meticulously inspect our surroundings for cleanliness as my mother did in those long-ago days. The "bugs" of worldliness and the "filth" of sin are not welcome on the highway that leads to glory.

I also remember through the eyes of a child the awesomeness of going through Dallas and Fort Worth—those big cities! In those days, there was no loop around town, so all travelers were forced to journey through the downtown district. I was frightened by all the traffic and the people and the tall buildings.

My little brother was fascinated and would constantly cry out, "Look, Daddy, look!" or "Oh, look, Daddy, look at the red horse!" (It was the famous flying red horse, the trademark of the Magnolia Oil Company, flying atop the tallest building in Dallas at the time, the Magnolia Building.) We were always thrilled to see the "flying red horse," because our dad worked for this famous company.

I also remember what my dad said: "I can't look, son. I can't be distracted, or I'll make a wrong turn. I must keep my eyes on the highway signs to be able to find my way through the city."

I have remembered that statement in my journey of life. If I let my eyes be distracted by the glamour of the world around me, I will, without a doubt, get on a wrong road. I must constantly watch the road signs and the road map. God has given us road signs and a road map—His Word, the Bible.

Memories of those long-ago days bring to mind how secure I felt on the journey. Even though we encountered many obstacles along the way, I was blissfully secure in the knowledge that my dad had everything under control.

Our journey through life may take many unknown turns, but if we are secure in the knowledge that our heavenly Father will take us safely through, there is no adverse circumstance that will be able to shake our absolute trust in Him.

At Grandmother's house, when we saw her standing with open arms to receive us, all the inconveniences of the journey faded away—the bugs and filth of the tourist courts, the scary detours, the frightening big cities. We knew it had been worth it all. Our journey through life may not always be pleasant, but the anticipation of the end of the journey at the Father's house makes it all worthwhile.

On the road to Grandmother's house! The Travis Nevels Family. Mr. and Mrs. Travis Nevels, Marceal, and Travis II. Year approximately 1940.

Questions with 3 No Answers

The most puzzling question that comes to Christian people at a time of great sorrow is, "Why?" There is no use in saying we ought not to ask, because we all do. We may never find the answer to that question because most of us look for it in the wrong place.

When bad things happen to us, we turn our thoughts inward, examining our past life for a possible reason. If we reflect backward on the life of Joseph, however, from the time he was sold into slavery by his brothers, we find no reason for the trials to which he was subjected. Only by looking forward in his life do we find the answer. God was preparing the way for Joseph to become a great leader and deliver to his people.

Joseph's Christ-like spirit in returning good for evil was manifested in his words to his brothers when they asked his forgiveness: "But as for you, ye thought evil against me: but God meant it unto good, to bring to pass, as it is this day, to save much people alive" (Genesis 50:20). Joseph was aware that God allowed the trials because He was able to use them for His purpose and knew that the ultimate outcome would be good.

In addition, if we look backward from the Cross we cannot see the Resurrection, the Ascension, and the birth of the church. Only by looking forward do we see God's reasons for the Cross. "Looking unto Jesus the author and finisher of our faith; who for the joy that was set before him endured the cross . . ." (Hebrews 12:2). The joy came after the Cross, not before.

Similarly, the reason for present trials and afflictions in our lives may not lie in our past but in our future. Only God knows what lies ahead. He can see the end of our life and knows what we need along life's way.

When we find ourselves maimed and broken by the crushing blows of life, we derive no comfort in looking back. Constant brooding on the irrevocable is unhealthy. No matter if we see a thousand things that might have changed the situation, it cannot now be changed.

We may find ourselves fighting against God if we fail to realize that He has had His hand in all our past. Of course, this does not mean that we lack freedom of choice or that we do not have responsibility. Indeed, we are to change adverse situations when possible, but on the other hand, we must accept what we cannot control as coming by the permission of God.

Afflictions of life seem to bring an awareness and an appreciation of little things we so often take for granted: a loving family, a beautiful day, a few hours of freedom from pain, a good job. There is an old saying: "We never appreciate health until there's sickness; nor affluence until there's poverty; nor life until there's death."

❋ *God Never Changes* ❋

As we study the change points of life, one thing must be clear in our minds: God never changes; He is immutable. His creation changes, by seasons and by time, but God is ever the same. "Jesus Christ the same yesterday, and to day, and for ever" (Hebrews 13:8). "I am the LORD, I change not" (Malachi 3:6).

Man lives in time, is a creation of God, and is subject to the changes caused by time. God, however, lives outside His creation in a timeless and changeless eternity. His nature never changes, His moral attributes never change, and His Word never changes. He is consistent. What He did and said yesterday agrees with what He says and does today.

Man was made in the image of God; therefore, his moral attributes (such as integrity, loyalty, and trustworthiness) should not change through circumstances of life.

When we are born again we acquire a new nature, God's nature, a nature that never changes. The new nature does not replace our old nature but dwells alongside our carnal human nature to subdue it. Consequently, we have a dual nature. The holy nature of God and the sinful human nature begin a tug of war for mastery in our lives.

Although the Spirit of God in our hearts hates sin and shrinks from it, our Adamic nature with its sinful tendencies is still very much alive and is attracted by the allure of the world. If we suppress God's Spirit and allow our own human nature to have mastery in our lives, then come forth carnal desires, old habits, "pity parties," and sinful tendencies. As we walk with the Lord and learn to yield to Him day by day, the old carnal nature becomes less powerful. When circumstances in our life change, God's nature (which does not change) living within will carry us through to victory.

• *Change Defined* •
The dictionary definition of the word change is:

1. *to make different*
2. *to alter*
3. *to lay aside*
4. *to substitute*
5. *to exchange*
6. *to lay aside something in favor of something else*
7. *the substitution of one thing for another*

Change means losing something in order to gain something else. We lay aside one thing in favor of something else. It is an exchange.

When the death of a loved one occurs, when health fails, when we lose our job and finances vanish away—how can we accept it and lay it aside in favor of another way of life? Yet this is what life is—constantly changing circumstances, questions with no answers.

• *Inner Fears* •
Some change points of life are not sad but represent a change in lifestyle. To be sure, when these changes occur, we lay aside one thing in favor of something else; we exchange; our life is altered. Here are examples:

1. *Marriage* (loss of independence—must consider someone else)
2. *Birth of baby* (oh, how lifestyle changes!)
3. *New job (pressure)*
4. *Change of career* (can I adapt?)

5. *Going to college* (new demands)

Not everyone has suffered the grief of losing a loved one through death, but all of us have suffered grief through loss. Most of us can relate to one or more of the following change points of life that are losses:

1. *Divorce* (loss of self-esteem, financial security, two full-time parents for children; rejection
2. *Loss of job* (loss of self-worth; financial security; fear of losing spouse's respect and understanding)
3. *Wayward children* (wrong crowd, drugs, alcohol, teenage pregnancy)
4. *Moving* (if forced to downgrade lifestyle)
5. *Loss of past relationship* (due to desertion, rejection, divorce, or terminal illness of spouse, parent, or child)
6. *Children leaving home* (empty-nest syndrome)
7. *Retirement* (if not planned)
8. *Loss of health* (self, child, parent, or spouse)
9. *Aging parents* (parent-child relationship reversed)
10. *Death of loved one* (spouse, child, parent, brother, sister, grandparent, or friend)

These change points bring many questions, such as these:

- Why did I lose my job?
- Why are we being forced to sell our home and find something cheaper?

- Why did my husband suddenly decide he didn't love me anymore and move out?
- Why did my son (daughter) turn to drugs?
- Why am I having to place my parent in a nursing home?
- Why does my child have this crippling disease?
- Why did my loved one die?

With these and many more questions we ask, "Why?" They are questions that may not have answers, at least not in this life.

In 1988, my dad, the anchor of my life, was diagnosed as having Alzheimer's disease. Alzheimer's disease is a degenerative brain disease, a form of dementia, and the fourth leading cause of death of American adults. It is tragic for family members as well as the victim.

As the disease progresses, there is no hope of recovery of memory, but people do not consist of memory alone. People have feelings, imaginations, desires, drives, will, and moral being. It is in these realms that we must try to touch Dad today.

Eighty-seven years old, Dad is now in a nursing home, bedfast, and must be fed through a feeding tube in the stomach. Some days he recognizes me after I tell him my name, while other days he stares vacantly and asks, "Who are you?" Nothing I say to him jars a responsive chord in his memory.

Alzheimer's disease is a cruel disorder, leaving bone and flesh intact while erasing judgment and memory.

This is one of the times when I ask, "Why?" This is one of the questions with no answers.

Within a family, dealing with questions that have no

answers means not only coping with your own frustrations and inadequacies but also watching those same feelings manifest themselves in family members. My own feeling of despair over Dad's situation is mirrored in my mother's devastation. Married sixty-four years, they are both suffering from the personal tragedy of Alzheimer's disease, which is the dissolution of self. How do I comfort her?

Another question with no answer.

In March 1981 when my granddaughter, Ashley Paige Camp, died suddenly at the age of six months, I thought I could not live through my own despair. Seeing the devastation of my son, Steve, and daughter-in-law, Pam, was like a cruel double blow. How do I comfort them?

Another question with no answer.

Coping with my own grief at my husband's death was monumental, yet it seemed more than I could possibly survive when I also witnessed the grief of my children. How do we survive grief? How do we comfort those who grieve?

More questions with no answers.

Not finding any answers makes us prisoners of our own fears and anxieties. In order to preserve our sanity, we must find ways to let go of the questions and disabling emotions, to accept our situation, and to go forward.

But how?

Every person, at one time or another, must cope with inner fear, and in coping with fear, we can choose to live our life in one of three ways:

> 1. We can flee our fears by fleeing reality. Feeling inadequate in the face of life-changing events, many people refuse to face facts. Shrinking from reality by refusing to find solutions to life's

problems is a form of escapism. By not facing fears, we are doomed to be imprisoned by them.

2. We can attempt to drown our fears in a whirl of escaping anything that might cause any pain. Living this way, a person constantly seeks to make life simply fun and games. We cannot solve the deep problems of life by pushing them aside in this form of escapism. Running from pain by chasing after pleasure is the way of the world, not the way of the Christian.

3. We can face our fears. This is the right way, and the only way to achieve peace of mind. When we face reality, look those questions with no answers straight in the eye, we will begin to find ways to accept the difficult times of life and move on.

But how?

There is a certain process of letting go that follows a definite pattern, and we will examine it in the following chapters. The questions with no answers are still there, but we can find ways to understand our emotions and to accept our situation.

Cecil Camp
May 25, 1927—June 2, 1986

Mr. and Mrs. Travis Nevels (author's parents)
1986—Before the onset of his Alzheimer's disease.

Travis Nevels, the author's father and anchor of
her life, recently lost his battle with Alzheimer's
disease. He passed from this life on March 27,
1994 at the age of 87 years.

God's Lent Child
Ashley Paige Camp
September 20, 1980—March 15, 1981

The Grief Process

Stages 1-3

I had survived my first year of widowhood and was well into my second when I first realized that grief is a process and follows a certain pattern. It wears many faces and has various stages with definite plateaus and climaxes.

Grief affects the physical being as well as the mental and emotional being. I lost fifteen pounds during my first two weeks of widowhood and ten more in the months that followed. I simply could not remember to eat.

I was sicker during that first year than I remember ever having been before. My body seemed unable to resist the disease germs. Grief seems to affect the immune system.

There were times during this period when I was sure I was dying—of a broken heart. There were times when I wanted to die, crying out to God to please take me home, too.

The dictionary definition of the word *grief* is "deep sadness caused by loss." It does not say what kind of loss—just loss. Any kind of loss can cause grief, not just the death of a loved one.

Perhaps you have experienced a loss such as I mentioned earlier (loss of job, divorce, sickness, and so on). The emotions described in the following chapters are some of the emotions you have felt during the grieving process connected with your loss. Perhaps you did not associate your various emotions with your grief, however.

The following discussion of the stages of grief should help all of us understand ourselves a little better, to understand that the feelings we have are normal, to understand that we are not monsters for having certain feelings. We are just frail mortals reacting to the difficult times in our lives.

Accepting the finality of separation is the ultimate goal of the grief process. The length of the various stages is not the same in everyone. The duration varies depending upon the individual and on the circumstance.

Those losing loved ones through long terminal illness experience emotions of grief throughout the illness as well as the death. Those losing loved ones suddenly and unexpectedly are confronted with an overwhelming situation all at one time. In the first instance, having experienced various stages of the grief process during the loved one's illness, the person is more prepared to accept the finality of separation at death than those in the second situation. The duration of the stages of grief may be different in these two cases; however, the emotions and feelings are the same.

The purpose of the grieving process is to accept the reality of what has happened and to begin to find new ways of filling up the emptiness caused by the loss. During this period, the bonds to the past are gradually loosened and the psychological attachment surrendered.

Through observation and actual experience, I found the

grieving process usually follows ten stages. Shifting in and out of these stages, a person will, most likely, experience all of them at one time or another during the grieving process.

• 1. Unbelief and Denial •

Usually, the first emotion we experience when faced with catastrophic change is unbelief and denial. These two are interchangeable and go hand in hand. At this point, the mind simply refuses to believe the facts.

Usually, the first statement someone makes when hearing tragic news is, "No! No! I don't believe it!" This was my reaction to the news that my baby grandaughter had died, my reaction when the doctor told me my dad had Alzheimer's disease, my reaction when my husband died: "No! Please, God, no!"

Denial protects us from the shock of unwelcome news and helps us control the way we finally receive and accept the facts. It is part of the way we adapt ourselves to ideas and events too horrible to comprehend all at once. We give our minds and emotions a chance to adjust, bit by bit, to the new information that might otherwise overwhelm us.

Many times following my husband's death, during this stage of my grief I would subconsciously pick up the phone and dial that familiar work number I had dialed so many times before. Only when an unfamiliar voice answered the phone did it register on my conscious mind that he was not there anymore.

On one such occasion, I was writing thank-you notes after the funeral. Needing the address of one of his relatives who had sent flowers, I snatched up the phone and dialed the number before I realized what I was doing.

Others have told me they have subconsciously flipped through greeting-card displays on holidays and special occasions with the notion of purchasing a card for their deceased loved one.

When the World Trade Center in New York was bombed in 1993, I listened to a doctor on the radio elaborate about the unbelief and denial process. He explained it as a "cushion" and said it was a helpmate to the survival of those trapped inside the building.

I have often wondered why survivors do not die of shock upon hearing tragic news. God, in His mercy, has built into us a "cushion."

In psychological terms, denial is a defense mechanism in which the person does not admit to himself consciously that painful facts exist. In other words, denial is a defense that acts as a buffer. It is good for us.

We must realize, however, that denying a problem will not make it go away. In fact, after a while denial actually compounds the problem. A person goes through normal denial in a relatively short period. But I have read of cases and am personally acquainted with one where exaggerated denial lasted many years.

Exaggerated denial is when a person refuses to let go of yesterday and insists on living in the past. I read of a woman who continued to set a place at the dinner table for her husband many years after his death. I read of another woman who has never given up her husband although he died ten years ago. She does not invite people to her home. She pretends he is still there and frequently talks to him.

I know a couple who lost their seventeen-year-old son in a tragic auto accident. For many years they kept his room exactly as he had left it. Clothes he had taken off were on the bed. Items he had taken from his pockets were lying on the dresser. Books and records were strewn around as he had left them. When people walked into the room, they got the impression that at any moment he would return.

This kind of morbid, exaggerated denial is extremely unhealthy to a person's mental stability.

• *2. Numbness* •

Initial denial is replaced by numbness. In this stage, the brain actually seems paralyzed, and even normal functions of life are not possible. Thought processes are numbed. It is impossible to make even small decisions. That is the reason experts tell us a grieving person should not make a major decision for at least one year. Decisions that cause a drastic change in lifestyle are traumatic in themselves; when a grieving person attempts to make them, he or she can easily make the wrong decision. The person then feels regret in addition to grief.

In this stage of my grief, I would sometimes react with uncontrollable hysterics when faced with the smallest decision. My life had changed so drastically that I felt I could not cope with another change. What would have been molehills at any other time in my life, now overnight had mushroomed into mountains—a flat tire, a dead battery, a washing machine that refused to work, a lawn mower I could not start. Little things we face every day suddenly became catastrophes.

Normally, I would do whatever it took to correct the situation and go on with life. But now, I could not flow with even the normal events in everyday life. The slightest change was monumental.

I remember coming home from work one evening and finding my phone line dead. Panic-stricken, I drove pell-mell to my son's house. At any other time of life it would have gone unnoticed—an inconvenience, but not a life-threatening incident. My thought processes were paralyzed and numbed.

Thankfully, incompetence and dependency during a crisis are not permanent. They only mean we are part of the human race.

• *3. Confusion, Resentment, Anger, and Guilt* •

Numbness is replaced by a variety of feelings, such as confusion, resentment, bewilderment, depression, disappointment, frustration, guilt, and, yes, even anger.

My life was in total confusion and chaos. At times, I would realize that I had not been to bed for twenty-four hours or that a day or perhaps two had passed and I had forgotten to eat. My life had no order.

It seems strange that resentment would be part of the grieving process, yet it is true. Amid all the confusion of everyday life, resentment surfaces when problems arise. During bereavement there are many problems: financial problems, family problems, job-related problems, insurance problems. Most of all, there is the monumental task of trying to salvage your life from the scrap heap after it has been torn apart and uprooted. Feeling resentment and anger toward your deceased spouse for leaving you to face confusion alone is a natural stage in the grieving process.

Anger is a very human reaction to frustration and disappointment. It is a basic emotion that helps us survive. We tend to become angry when we feel frightened, hurt, or threatened.

If a wife has been totally dependent on her husband, this feeling of vulnerability may make her feel bitterness toward the deceased spouse for having "deserted" her. Becoming upset and angry under these circumstances is a reaction to tremendous frustration in the face of these life-changing events.

For example, Martha is a wife who has been accustomed to depending upon her husband for almost all her needs. And now, when she feels she needs him even more as she grows older, he is no longer there for her. Thus, Martha feels betrayed, disappointed, and fearful of being left alone. These feelings most often will trigger anger. Being aware of the true cause of her angry feelings and knowing how to cope with them will help Martha to understand herself.

To be sure, these angry feelings are not confined just to the death of a spouse. They can be triggered by any loss in our lives.

During a divorce, these same feelings surface. A wife not only feels deserted but also rejected. Rejection triggers feelings of worthlessness, which in turn trigger the display of anger.

Likewise, a wife can become angry at her husband at the loss of a job as finances vanish. She often vents all her frustrations and disappointments on him when it is probably not his fault.

Similarly, parents will sometimes feel resentful and angry when their children marry and leave home. Perhaps now that their own home life has been uprooted, they feel their closeness to the child has been threatened. There especially will be anger if the parents think the marriage is not suitable. Plans they have made for this child become shattered dreams to them, and unquestionably, shattered dreams trigger resentment and anger.

Another life-changing event that can cause anger is learning a son or daughter is hooked on drugs or alcohol. Or, how about an unmarried teenage daughter dropping the bombshell that she is pregnant?

This type of anger blends in with the emotion of guilt and self-blame. In these situations, parents sometimes ask themselves, "Where did I go wrong?" They blame themselves, and the emotion of guilt triggers the anger—anger toward the child, anger toward the situation, and often anger toward God for letting it happen.

Children, too, experience angry feelings when a parent dies or leaves the home as a result of divorce. They often feel frustrated, resentful, and unloved.

As a result, when Nancy got a divorce, her son buried his frustrations over losing his father behind a wall of anger. He was soon in trouble at school. Nancy at first blamed herself for depriving her son of his father. Eventually, time and others taught her to see that she had done her best and helped her to let go of self-blame and guilt. When she was able to do that, then her son was able to let go of his anger.

Many widows are also plagued by self-blame and guilt: "I knew he had a heart condition; I should have forced him to slow down." Or regrets: the cruise you never took, the fishing trips you never shared with him.

Experts suggest examining these feelings to see if they are reasonable. Ask yourself, "Could I have forced him to slow down?" or "Did he really want me along on the fishing trips?" Truthful answers can help us see that self-blame is at least exaggerated and in most cases unfounded.

In addition, when a spouse dies, it is natural for the survivor to struggle with the often unanswerable question, "Why did I survive?" Feelings of self-blame and guilt surface. "Survivor's guilt" is a psychological term for this phenomenon. The survivors have an irrational but persistent sense of guilt about having survived. These were my feelings—guilty for having survived and guilty because my children were deprived of their father, even though there was nothing I could have done to prevent it. Survivor's guilt prompts unjustified feelings of self-blame.

On the other hand, all survivors do not grieve intensely. There are those who have feelings of guilt for their lack of grief. Not all marriages are happy ones. Because death provided release and relief from an unbearable situation, some grieve over their lack of grief. Just because the intolerable situation is no longer a part of that person's life does not mean she doesn't feel loneliness. Indeed, she needs support to begin a new life alone.

Even though resentment, anger, and guilt are very much a part of grieving, they are disabling emotions. They usually subside in a relatively short period, to be replaced by the next stages in the grief process.

The Grief Process
Stages 4-6

• *4. Loss of Direction* •

Next comes a loss of direction in life, a sense of hopelessness, a sense of not caring. In this stage of the grieving process, nothing matters anymore. What once seemed important suddenly means nothing: home, job, possessions are meaningless. Days run together and have no meaning or sequence.

Nine months before my husband died, we moved into a beautiful new home. It was fun buying the land—a one-acre, wooded lot in a subdivision north of town. It was fun shopping for the "extras" and the "pretties." We had saved for new furniture—it was fun picking it out. But after Cecil's death, it was no longer fun. Our home became meaningless to me. It was only a shell housing painful memories.

One day, during this stage of my grief, my mother visited and innocently remarked that my flower beds looked neglected and ragged with their many weeds. "I don't care about flower beds and weeds!" I lashed out at her. "Nothing matters anymore!"

I responded with hopelessness, yet I knew God. How do those who do not know God survive the difficult times of life? The truth is that some of them do not survive. With no hope in this life nor in the one to come, when their world crumbles some turn to alcohol or drugs, some turn to crime, some desert their families, and some commit suicide. Perhaps it is in this stage of the grief process when these things occur.

A law officer I once worked with was called to the home of a suicide victim. When he arrived he discovered it to be the home of his friend. The friend's suicide note blamed a recent painful divorce for his actions. The note said, "Nothing matters anymore."

It is in this stage of the grieving process that the "loonies" emerge. This is my word for unusual ideas, practices, and compulsions.

One of my loonies was the compulsion I felt to stay at the cemetery. I spent hours just walking among the graves reading the inscriptions on the tombstone. I became acquainted with all the family plots and began to feel at home there. Scrutinizing each tombstone, I noted the ages of the men who had died. When I came across someone who had lived longer than Cecil, I felt cheated.

A friend of mine confessed that she went to the cemetery each day and "grave sat," talking to her deceased husband about the events of the day.

Writing notes became a compelling, all-consuming task. I didn't talk as my friend confessed to doing, but I did write. Writing was more comfortable than talking.

My husband's favorite shirt became my security blanket.

I slept with it under my pillow. Another friend told me that one of her loonies was sleeping in her deceased husband's pajamas.

In time, the loonies subsided and eventually disappeared. I no longer felt the compulsion to walk among the graves. In time, I put away the shirt and my pen became still and silent. The loonies did not mean that I was loony. They only meant I was reacting in my own way to the elusive, flitting frailty of life.

• *5. A Sense of Aloneness and Separation* •

During this stage of grief, a sense of aloneness and separation surfaces. At this point, people suffering from grief need to be in the midst of people. They feel alone and separated, as though no one cares and no one understands. This feeling intensifies if people avoid them. Many people, afraid of saying or doing the wrong thing, say nothing and do nothing. They simply avoid contact with the grieving person.

As a result, Sue, a new widow with two teenaged children, in frustration said, "We're not lepers! What we have is not contagious!"

In addition, the trauma of going from "happily married" to "suddenly single" is a shocking experience that no one can relate to except people who have lived through it. A widowed person senses that she does not fit in anymore. She feels alone. She does not relate to married couples because part of her is gone. Likewise, she does not relate to single people because she does not feel single. These feelings may cause her eventually to withdraw from society, thereby increasing her feelings of aloneness and separation.

Moreover, the person who led a happily married life and then is thrown into the throes of the suddenly single life faces a shock syndrome that those around her usually do not understand. She is often labeled as cold and withdrawn when actually she hurts as though she has undergone major surgery without an anesthetic. Part of her has been amputated, yet she is expected to carry on her life as before. She is forced by society to put on a happy face and go about her normal routine. I had to work in order to support myself, as many widows must do, and it became a daily ordeal to put up the front necessary to hold my job, knowing that the workplace was not the place to succumb to emotions and feelings.

Therefore, feelings are kept bottled up inside where they fester and corrupt and refuse to heal. An emotional wound must heal from the inside out, by our talking freely to someone who cares. The wound deepens and intensifies when feelings are locked inside. Grieving people need to talk about the sudden vacuum in their lives.

Remember Sue, the widow who felt like a leper? She, like most, pretended to others that all was well in order not to become a bore, while deep inside, suppressed emotions refused to heal. In order to make the transition easier for her two teenaged children, she kept her true feelings locked inside.

But, fortunately for Sue, she had a caring friend who, like a magnet, was able to draw out those bottled-up feelings. In the process, cleansing and healing occurred.

"What are you feeling today, Sue? I know you must be lonely without him. How are you adjusting? Would you like to talk?"

Sue's friend would draw her out with questions. What questions were asked was irrelevant. Sue responded, not to the questions, but to the sincerity of her friend.

Not so with Ellen. To Ellen, becoming suddenly single was the most devastating experience of her life. A few months after the death of her husband of thirty-one years, she began to look forward once again to Sunday and the anticipated fellowship not only with God but also with her brothers and sisters in the Lord.

"But," she complained, "Sunday is the loneliest day of my week." By nature a shy person, Ellen, not wanting to intrude into the world of couples and not feeling comfortable in the world of singles, would usually eat alone, and Sunday became a replay of the rest of her week.

"My life has changed so drastically," Ellen confessed. "I feel left out among married couples and feel that I don't fit in with the singles crowd either because I don't feel single."

In her aloneness and desperation, Ellen found herself silently screaming, "If only someone would mention his name! They act as if he never existed."

Ellen needed people and needed to feel that she still belonged, but in her self-imposed isolation she had removed herself from the warmth that others can give.

A person like Ellen will often withdraw into her own world, rarely reaching out or allowing others entry. Though she needs others, she may rebuff them if they try to get too close.

In this stage of aloneness and separation the grieving person may don a mask. A mask is used to cover, to conceal, to disguise.

Oh, the masks we wear to disguise our true feelings! We hide our worst, guard our best, and try to communicate on the middle ground of anonymity. Why?

We fear each other. We guard our wounds so as not to be hurt again. The vulnerable inner person retreats when masks are donned.

Loneliness is sometimes covered by loudness. A tender and disillusioned heart is concealed effectively behind a "don't care" attitude. A world that is falling apart lies quietly unseen behind the "all's well" mask.

When Sue's friend asked, "How are you, Sue?" her automatic response was "Fine," when deep inside her cry was, "My world is falling apart but no one seems to care." Unquestionably, Sue's friend did care. She was not a trained psychologist, but she was sensitive enough to read facial expressions, tone of voice, and vocal quality. She was able to strip away Sue's "all's well" mask by further probing, caring, and asking questions.

On the other hand, Ellen's "don't care" mask disguises her tender and wounded heart that recoils with the fear of being hurt again. She separates herself from her friends, hiding behind her mask while secretly crying in her heart, "If only someone would mention his name." She has attempted to shield herself from further hurt but, in the process, has shielded herself from love.

In order to minister to Ellen, sensitive friends must penetrate her facade by taking the initiative and inviting her for lunch, for shopping, for gabbing. Through their caring concern, Ellen may once again reach out to the warmth that others can give.

People in Ellen's situation often decline invitations or accept only to cancel at the last minute. They fear losing control of their emotions in front of others. They may even feel that if they have a good time they are being disloyal to their loved one's memory. Gentle encouragement will help them know it is all right to begin enjoying life again.

Going still further, Marianne is a loud, brash individual.

Her obnoxious attitude really covers loneliness, insecurities, and feelings of worthlessness brought on by a devastating divorce. The nonverbal component of a conversation with Marianne far outweighs the actual words spoken. To minister to her inner feelings caring friends must hear what is unspoken and see what is unseen. By listening to the nonverbal aspects of speech—volume, pitch, rate, and vocal quality—rather than the actual words spoken, we can tell whether or not Marianne is nervous, depressed, or happy.

What message would we get if someone said to us, "I love you" in the same tone of voice he might say, "It's ten o'clock"? More than likely, we would discount the actual words spoken and instead pick up on the indifferent quality of vocal expression. Similarly, Marianne may be loud with her words, but her vocal quality, tonal expression, and facial language speak an instinctive message that cannot be silenced.

Being able to minister to the wounded spirits of people like Marianne, Sue, and Ellen rather than merely responding to their masks is truly a Christ-like attribute. Jesus Himself looked beyond the facade and ministered to the real need.

• 6. A Desire to Be Happy Again •

Quietly one day, with no bells and no fanfare, a new balance will begin to return. It will not be the same as before; nevertheless, it will be the beginning of an internal equilibrium—the beginning of healing—the desire to be happy again. Active, daily, all-consuming mourning slowly ebbs away and we begin the journey back from grief.

My grief took on the likeness of a cocoon, shielding me from life. I hurt so deeply that I retreated into my cocoon for protection against any further hurt. I shielded myself from hurt but also from happiness. When I sensed that first flickering ray of hope, that beginning of an internal equilibrium, the desire to be happy again, I realized that only as I forced myself from this cocoon could I begin to live again.

The beautiful emperor moth escapes from its cocoon through a very small hole, leaving the cocoon intact. It is only with much struggle that it squeezes its body through the tiny opening, but when it does so, it comes forth with beautifully developed, gigantic wings and soars into the heavens.

If someone, however, should see the helpless insect struggling to escape and attempt to lessen its struggles by enlarging the hole, it would come forth with its swollen, squatty body dragging its underdeveloped, shriveled wings, doomed to be stunted all its life. The pressure to which the moth's body is subjected in passing through the narrow opening is God's provision for forcing the juices of the body into the vessels of the wings. Only through struggle does it develop to its full potential.

So it is with humanity. Only through the trials and struggles of life do we develop to our full potential. In this stage of grief when a desire for happiness begins, by emerging from the cocoon, even slowly, a person begins the journey back from grief.

The Grief Process
Stages 7-10

• 7. Knowing That You must Relinquish the Past •

Holding on to the past intensifies and prolongs grief. Letting go means accepting reality, allowing things to fall into their proper prospective, and admitting powerlessness: "I cannot bring back the past; I must accept things as they are in the present."

In order to be happy again, we must relinquish the past. In every new experience, whether happy or sad, there is a need to let go of what was. Until we do, we cannot appreciate what is. We grow by losing and leaving and letting go. God has designed it so.

Letting go is something all of us do, whether consciously or subconsciously. We grow up, get married, have children, move to new neighborhoods, win promotions, lose jobs. Our parents grow old, our children grow up and leave the nest, our loved ones die. Only as we relinquish and let go of what once was can we go on to what can be—not forgetting the past, but letting go of the past. There is a difference. We can cherish our memories, but not live in them.

In this stage of grief, we know in our heart that if we are to be happy again we must let go and relinquish the past. But knowing is not the same as doing. We know, but seem to hold more tightly instead of relaxing our grip. The unknown future seems scary since the known past has been so chaotic. We hold to the confused past instead of walking into the unknown future.

Assuredly, saying goodbye to a past life is part of every transition. When my friend's daughter, Millie, left for college, my friend mentioned to Millie that she might turn her bedroom into a sewing room. Millie reacted in a strange way. "No!" she cried, "I need my room!" What Millie was really saying was, "I'm not ready yet to let go of my childhood home."

As time passed, one day Millie said to her mother, "Oh, by the way, Mom, if you still want to do something with my room, go ahead." In her own time and in her own way, Millie had let go.

So it is with us. In our own time and in our own way, we too will let go. The important thing is to give ourselves time. We will know in our own hearts when we have made that transition. Letting go is not betraying the past but having faith in the future.

• *8. Gradually Letting Go* •

In this stage of grief, I found that the more I would reach out to others, the easier it became to let go. I learned that when I would venture from my shell and become more involved with the hurts of others, the protective shell of grief would melt away. Reaching to help others, I was helped instead.

In the following true story about a flop-eared mouse, you will see that when I reached out to minister to the hurts of my children, I too was helped. By helping others, we help ourselves.

• *The Flop-Eared Mouse* •

"To appoint unto them that mourn . . . to give unto them beauty for ashes, the oil of joy for mourning . . ." (Isaiah 61:3).

I sighed, slowly unlocked the front door, and then slipped quietly inside. Still unaccustomed to coming home from work to the stillness of an empty house, I felt the sting of hot tears as self-pity engulfed me.

Trying to keep body and soul together these last six months had not been easy. With widowhood had come the awareness of new responsibilities. But now, with Christmas approaching, I was suddenly overwhelmed. I yearned for all I had lost and wanted to run away from new responsibilities.

Living alone was frightening. Oh, the children lived near and visited often, yet they did not understand that I was scared—scared of being alone, scared of the future, scared of finances. Oh, God, I can't even buy them Christmas presents this year. Yes, self-pity was becoming a constant companion.

Just a few days before, Joy, my youngest, had asked, "Mama, aren't you going to put up the Christmas decorations?"

"No, baby, I don't think so. I don't feel up to Christmas this year."

"But, Mama," she wailed, "we must have decorations. Daddy would have wanted us to. Presents don't matter, but please, Mama, put up the decorations." Half-heartedly, I had promised.

Now, memories of happier Christmases dogged my footsteps as I trudged listlessly up the stairs to the attic. Finding the boxes containing the decorations amid the disarray proved to be a more difficult task than I had at first assumed.

Rummaging in the dark corners illuminated only by the dim rays of a flashlight, I stumbled over a forgotten chest. Hastily brushing away cobwebs, dust, and what felt like squirmy things (but in the light of the flashlight proved to be only balls of dust), I gingerly lifted the lid.

Then, as if by magic, the attic was instantly transformed as Christmases past came to life and paraded in review, recalling nostalgic squeals of delighted children. Out of the chest came baby dolls, footballs, baseballs, catchers' mitts, Barbie dolls (complete with clothes and high-heeled shoes), tiny cars, a Raggedy Ann doll, stuffed animals, and rag dolls. Eagerly, I lifted each one. Oh, here's Steve's first toy train complete with locomotive and track! I was as excited as a child on Christmas morning as I gently unpacked favorite toys of long ago.

Then, I saw it—the flop-eared mouse. Twenty-six years old, there it lay, forgotten, at the bottom of the chest—one button eye gone, the other held together by a safety pin, its gray fur rubbed off where tiny hands had lovingly caressed. We called it the "security mouse." From a toddler to a teenager, Joy had made this little creature her constant companion. I brushed away a tear as I gently picked up the limp, floppy body.

Thank You, Lord, I silently prayed. You have shown me what to do for my children at Christmas.

Christmas Day dawned bright and clear. I was nervous and apprehensive, yet expectant. What would their reaction be?

Steve and his family arrived first. Anxiously, I searched the face of this man, my son, as he beheld the many brightly colored Christmas decorations.

I was not disappointed as his eyes mirrored first amazement and then wonder. Then the little boy of long ago raced across the room and began laughing and crying all at the same time as he picked up a broken bat, a deflated football, a well-worn catcher's mitt, and a tiny car (minus one wheel). His thirty-year-old train, sitting resplendent on its track, circled the room. As I watched him wipe away the tears, I knew he was remembering Christmases of long ago when he had received these same toys and his dad had said, "Come on, son; let me pitch you some balls."

Vicki came in next, my eldest. Hesitantly tiptoeing in, her eyes were wide and filled with wonder. I watched as she cradled baby dolls and Barbie dolls and Raggedy Ann. Tears fell unchecked as she gently stroked her favorite toy, a stuffed Pluto dog. Thirty-six years old, its nap was gone and its ears hung limp; nevertheless, I heard her say softly, "My dog."

"Hey, Maw," Tracy, her seventeen-year-old, said to me, "where did the antique catcher's mask come from?"

Steve said, "I'll have you know, young man, that's the finest catcher's mask made."

"Looks antique to me," Tracy muttered.

Then Joy arrived.

Amid the noise, confusion and laughter, her squeals could be heard above it all. "My mouse! My mouse! Where did you find my mouse?" Then clutching the little critter around its limp, floppy neck, she danced it around the room as she had done in those long-ago childhood days.

When the day ended my children said, "Mama, you couldn't have given us a happier Christmas."

That was five Christmases ago, and I guess we have started a family tradition. Every Christmas now I unpack the chest and display the favorite toys of bygone years: dolls, stuffed animals, toy cars, balls, bats, gloves, the toy train, Barbie, Raggedy Ann, Pluto dog, and, of course, the flop-eared mouse.

My grandchildren have started adding their favorites to our collection. Last year on Christmas Eve little Katie, my five-year-old granddaughter, slipped something into my hands. "Look, Maw, this is for your Christmas box."

"Yes, honey," I laughed, "it certainly belongs there." It was her favorite baby doll, limp and bedraggled, with hair stiff and sticking in all directions and two of its fingers missing.

As I cradled her contribution, I silently prayed, "Thank You, Lord, for the lesson I have learned. Thank You for showing me that when I forget myself and reach out to bring happiness to others then You allow the healing balm of Your Spirit to turn 'mourning into joy.' Thank You for giving me 'beauty for ashes' in the form of a flop-eared mouse."

Could it be, I wondered, that when the wise men brought gifts to the Christ child on that first Christmas, they included a soft, furry, flop-eared mouse for tiny hands to caress? In my imagination I like to think that they did.

• 9. Gently Closing the Door on the Past •

Closing the door on the past is a necessary stage in the

grieving process. People who do well after catastrophic loss are those who can perceive the good in what is left of their lives and those who realize the necessity of creating a new reality from the shattered pieces of life. It will not be the same life, because that life is over, but it can still be a beautiful life.

Another way of looking at this stage of the grieving process is to understand the tasks a person must accomplish:

1. The first is to accept the reality of the loss.
2. The second is to experience the pain of grief. Some people try to experience grief without pain, but there is pain in the severing of any relationship. Some people try to alleviate the pain with medication or alcohol, but anytime drugs or alcohol are used, little grieving can be done at that time. Others try to eliminate pain by traveling. But whenever they come home, the grief is still there. Grieving can be delayed, but it can never be eliminated. It is best to face the pain head-on and take it one day at a time.
3. The third task is to adjust to an environment without who or what has been lost.
4. The last task is to withdraw emotional energy and reinvest it in something else, another activity or another relationship. This step goes back to the definition of change: "to substitute; to exchange; to lay aside something in favor of something else; the substitution of one thing for another."

Reinvesting emotional energy is the art of exchanging "grave clothes" for "resurrection clothes." At Easter time, the dull, drab, dead-looking countryside changes its garment. The trees, flowers, and shrubs are now clothed with beautiful new green leaves and flowers. The seemingly dead has come alive! The resurrection is real! What was once dead has put on a new body and is alive! In the springtime, nature attests to the resurrection.

Jesus said, "I am the resurrection, and the life: he that believeth in me, though he were dead, yet shall he live: and whosoever liveth and believeth in me shall never die" (John 11:25-26).

When we close the door on the past, shedding the dull, drab, dead-looking clothing of grief, we change into a radiant garment of new life. Closing the door on the past attests to the resurrection. What was seemingly dead radiates new life.

When we can honestly pray, "Lord, help me to gently close the door on the past, to cherish all my memories, but once again to live," then we have moved to the final stage of the journey back from grief—acceptance.

• *10. Acceptance* •

When we can remember a loss with a little detachment and much less pain, we have accepted the loss and mourned it fully. We accept that life is different now and move on.

When acceptance comes, we can march bravely forward to whatever God has in store, knowing that He is the Captain of our soul. He cares about each hurt and joy we experience.

Accepting my loss has been easier when I remember

certain things. One such incident is recalling an experience of prayer. On May 17, 1986, two weeks before Cecil died, while I was praying I felt God speak to me. The words He said seemed foreign as they did not match our present circumstances. Puzzled, I wrote them down. When God took Cecil home on June 2, 1986, two weeks later, I then realized the significance of God's words.

These are the words the Lord spoke to me as I recorded them on paper that day:

> My child, do not be in distress, for I love you and hear your cries. As you draw close to Me, the everlasting arms of comfort will envelop you. Trust in My timing, for My ways are not your ways. Let My peace rule in your heart.

The most significant words to me were, "Trust in My timing." God's timing is always right. Sometimes we do not want to accept His timing, but He makes no mistakes; He is always right.

Other painful memories have allowed me to see the handiwork of God in the events of life. These painful memories have helped me to trust my future implicitly to God's hands. If He cared about me in my yesterdays, He will carry me through today and into my tomorrows.

At the funeral, Pastor Spears's message was on the "Thirteenth Hour." He said we have only twelve hours in the day (our life), and we must accomplish God's will in our allotted time. It might seem to us that Cecil's death was an untimely one since he was only fifty-nine, but God's timing is never wrong. He accomplished his mission on earth and fulfilled God's purpose for his life in his allotted twelve hours. God does not give us "extra" time—he does not give us the "thirteenth hour."

Trust in My timing—trust in My timing!

The night before Cecil died, God allowed all three of our children to phone and then to come out to see us. I wondered about this at the time because it was very strange. It is almost impossible for all of us to get together even when we try to plan it, but nevertheless, one by one, they came. Steve came first, then Vicki, then Joy. We had a fun time that night—we grilled hamburgers, made home-made ice cream, and played Trivial Pursuit. A loving heavenly Father allowed all three of my children to spend a fun evening with their dad on his last night on earth. It is hard not to question God's timing, but looking back, I can see the handiwork of God in the events of my life. He is a loving God!

When I learned to find something constructive in my experience, I knew I had said my goodbyes, accepted my new reality, and moved on, turning the grief of futility and despair into faith and hope and release.

The 7 Angels

After prayer meeting one night my friend Glenda remarked to me, "I sure am tired of living here."

"Here in Longview?" I inquired.

"No, here on earth. I long for my eternal home."

In thinking about that statement, I am convinced that she is right. Our ties should not be to temporal things but to eternal things. The more we become involved in the things of this world, the less we will long for the other world. The more we let go and relinquish on earth, the greater will be our yearning for the eternal. Unhindered by ties of this world, we will have greater ability to hear the beckoning call of the angels at heaven's open door.

• Seeing the Unseen •

"While we look not at the things which are seen, but at the things which are not seen: for the things which are seen are temporal; but the things which are not seen are eternal" (II Corinthians 4:18).

God wants us to yearn for and to seek what is unseen—the eternal things of God. There is a place in God where He allows our spirit to "see." There are things that we "know"—not by what our natural eye beholds but by what our spiritual eye beholds.

When God breathed into Adam the breath of life, He breathed in something of Himself. Man is unique. He is different from the animals, for in his bosom resides something created in the image of God Himself, which is called the human spirit.

It is not by our natural senses that we know there is a God, even though we can see, hear, and touch the beauty of His creation. It is not by our mind, will, and emotions that we know God, even though we can reason that there must be a Higher Power. It is only by our spirit (the part of us that is like God) that we can recognize and know God.

God speaks to us through our spirit. We "hear" Him with our spirit. It is in our spirit that we experience conviction, repentance, and then a merging of our human spirit with God's Holy Spirit as He comes to live within. As we learn to yield to that unseen Guide day by day, He allows us to "see" and to "know" the unseen—the eternal.

When there is sickness, the eyes of faith "see" healing. When there is despair, the eyes of hope "see" peace. When there is death, the eyes of the resurrected Christ living within "see" life beyond the grave.

During my grief, I found that when I confronted painful memories and laid myself bare before the Lord, those memories, even though painful, had a therapeutic effect. They helped to dispel gloom and foreboding as cleansing and healing began.

One such painful memory that has helped to heal the wounds is recalling the circumstances of a dream that my husband, Cecil Camp, had five years before his death when God allowed him to glimpse "unseen" things.

It was May 1981, and Cecil had a dream that greatly disturbed him. He was crying as he told it to me the next morning. Shaking, he also told it to our pastor and to our children. He dreamed that he died very suddenly. Immediately, his spirit left his body and he hovered overhead looking down at his body.

He saw many people scurrying about frantically trying to revive him—doctors, nurses, technicians—hooking him up to life-support machines. He could see me, his three children (Vicki, Steve, and Joy), Pastor Spears, and people from our church. All of us were crying.

He said he kept calling to us, "Hey, here I am, up here! Look up here. I'm all right. I'm okay. Look up here!"

But none of us could hear him.

All at once, he began rising. Higher and higher he climbed, the ones below becoming smaller and smaller, until we were no longer visible. Suddenly, he broke through what seemed an invisible barrier to the most breathtaking place he had ever seen. He forgot about us below as he began to explore this captivating new place.

Soon, he felt a tug and began to go down, down, down, until he realized he was going back into his body. He began to cry out to the Lord, "No, no, I don't want to go back! I want to go on to that beautiful place to be with You."

But the Lord spoke to him and said, "In a little while you can come, but not now. Your work is not quite finished. Soon you will be with Me. What you have seen is only a glimpse, a foretaste."

And then he woke up. Cecil spoke about this dream many times over the years, describing as best he could the beauty and wonders he had seen. In his frustration of trying to describe it, he summed it up in hopelessness by saying, "I'm sorry. There are just no such words in the English language."

My husband of thirty-eight years died exactly as he had seen in the dream God had given him five years before. I believe that when the artery ruptured, his spirit began leaving his body and hovered overhead awhile, as in the dream. I believe he saw the doctors and the nurses feverishly hooking up the life-support system, as in the dream.

I believe he saw his family gathered there weeping and praying, as in the dream. I believe he saw his pastor and friends keeping vigil with his family all night, as in the dream. I believe he was saying to us, "Hey, here I am. I'm up here! Look up here. I'm all right. I'm okay. Look up here!"

Just as surely as Cecil died the way he had dreamed five years before, I believe the rest of the dream is true, too. I believe that when God reached down and stopped the heartbeat, Cecil's spirit ascended to that beautiful place where there is no more pain, no more sorrow, no more tears, where the Lamb is the light!

Remembering Cecil's glimpse of God's secret things has helped to make my grief more bearable. I know that if the Lord loved Cecil enough to give him a foretaste of the wonders of heaven, then He loves me enough to heal the memories and the wounds made by grief.

Thank You, Lord, for loving us!

Another experience of "seeing the unseen" follows.

• *The Angels* •

"And he dreamed, and behold a ladder set up on the earth, and the top of it reached to heaven: and behold the angels of God ascending and descending on it" (Genesis 28:12).

I have been reluctant to share my slory of the angels because some do not believe in supernatural visitations. Nonetheless, the unbelief of some does not alter the fact that it did happen. Therefore, I would like to share the following true narrative.

Will I ever "see" them again? Are they with me right now? Oh, I like to think that they are. The angels. So many things have happened since that day. So many things—so many things.

Because of what lay ahead, God sent ministering angels to me. Looking back in retrospect, I see the handiwork of God, and I recognize His intervention in the circumstances of my life. I recognize His loving concern for me. Thank You, Lord Jesus, for loving me!

It was while I was praying at home alone one day that God led me through a day in His courts. At that time, my husband, Cecil, and I were going through a particularly low point in our lives. His health was failing. We had had financial reverses. I was at a low, low ebb, so I prayed . . . and prayed. Prostrate on the floor of our small study, my face buried in the carpet, I sobbed to God.

Then, deep within my spirit, God spoke to me. "Look up," said He.

I lifted my face from the carpet.

"What do you see?" He asked.

"Nothing," I weakly murmured.

"Look at the sofa. What do you see?"

"Nothing."

"Look at the black chair." I looked.

"What do you see?"

"Nothing."

"Look at the chair behind the desk," He continued. "What do you see?"

"Nothing."

"You are right," the Lord continued, speaking to my amazed and frightened heart. "You see nothing with your natural eyes, but seated there are three angels that I have sent to protect, to comfort, and to minister to you. For a little while, I am going to let you sense their presence. You will be able to 'see' them—not with your natural eye, but with your spiritual eye."

When the Lord finished this unusual discourse, suddenly I "saw." One was seated on the sofa, one on the black chair, and one behind the desk, as He had said. I was observing through my "spiritual eyes," through the deepest perception of my spirit, the kindest faces I had ever witnessed. Strength, security, and power exuded and emanated from them—three ministering angels dispatched by God to comfort one of His confused and hurting children!

Then, just as suddenly, they were gone!

Planning to drive to the bank for Cecil in the early afternoon, I hurried through my morning chores. The hum of the dishwasher and whirr of the vacuum no longer mingled with jangled nerves. The new-found peace in my heart was an exhilarating change for my troubled spirit!

After lunch, as I climbed behind the wheel of my car, suddenly, they were there again! The angels! One was sitting beside me in the front seat, one was in the back seat, and lo and behold, the third was on the hood of my car!

Slowly I backed out of the driveway, not really knowing what to do. I put the car in drive and started the fifteen-mile trip to the bank located in the neighboring town of Kilgore, Texas. The angels and I! I was more than a little frightened. I had never been accompanied by three guardian angels before! Or had I?

So away we went! One in the front seat, one in the back seat, and the other on the hood of the car! Zipping in and out of traffic on the highway, I grinned to myself as I could imagine the havoc if other drivers could also "see" the angel on the hood of the car. What a day!

Swinging into a parking space at the bank, I opened my door and got out. The angels got out. Not knowing what to expect, I walked into the bank. The angels followed. As I went to the loan officer to transact my husband's business, one sat in the seat next to me, one stood beside me, and the other stood behind me. Thank You, Lord, for loving me.

Business over, we started home—the angels and I. One on the front seat, one on the back seat, and one on the hood of the car!

By this time, my fright had subsided somewhat, and I now felt secure and protected and was thoroughly enjoying my day. Nearing home, I swung by my husband's place of business to tell him of the outcome of my transaction at the bank.

As I stepped from the car, my supernatural visitors did too. I walked into the office. So did they. As I sat down on the couch, one sat down beside me. Then, of all things, Cecil sat down too, barely missing the angel! Seeing the horrified look on my face, he exclaimed, "Whatever is the matter with you?"

"Oh, nothing, just a little nervous, I guess," I managed to stammer. My heart was pounding! My mind was racing! Should I tell him about the angels? Would they leave if I said anything?

I kept silent.

"Come on," Cecil said, "let's go get some coffee."

Getting into the car, one sat between us, one sat in the back seat, and the other sat on the hood of the car (where else?). I have wondered many times over the years since then about my extraordinary hood ornament. Is he riding on my car today? I like to think that he is.

We slid into a booth in the coffee shop. My thoughts were spinning. Oh-oh! Watch out! You're going to sit on him! Watch out!

As we drank our coffee and talked, I would, from time to time, sneak a surreptitious glance at the supernatural visitor sitting across from me. My husband, noticing my strange behavior, snapped, "For heaven's sake, what's wrong with you now? What are you looking at?" Still afraid that my angels would disappear if I acknowledged them, I made a lame excuse.

We left the coffee shop and headed home after dropping Cecil off at his office—one on the front seat, one on the back seat, and one on the hood of the car! As we pulled into the driveway and I got out of the car, just as suddenly as they had come the angels were gone.

Later that evening as I was telling Cecil of our supernatural visitation, he, listening in amazement, laughed about almost sitting in an angel's lap. "I thought you were cracking up in the coffee shop," he confessed. "You kept staring at something so intently."

God works in mysterious ways. His ways are not our

ways, His Word declares. I have not felt or sensed the presence of the angels since that day, but I think about them often and wonder if they are nearby.

So many things have happened since that day—heart attacks, open-heart surgery, and death.

Remembering God's protective angels, I found the strength to face life after the death of our little grand-daughter, Ashley Paige Camp. She was our son's only child and the apple of his eye. What do we say to the devastated parents? The Lord does help us to comfort them.

The memory of God's angels carried me through the dark days of watching my husband, Cecil, endure crippling heart attacks and open-heart surgery.

Then on June 2, 1986, my world collapsed as my husband of thirty-eight years was suddenly taken from me. God called His faithful servant home to glory. But what about me, Lord? How do I go on? My heart is crushed!

The memory of God's protection and God's love for me has been my undergirding strength. I believe in guardian angels, and I believe that God dispatched three from the glory world just for me! Thank You, Lord, for caring for me!

Cecil Camp and son, Steve.

Cecil and Marceal Camp with granddaughter, Katie Camp Easter, 1986 (six weeks before Cecil's death—his last picture)

Merceal and daughters, Vicki Gatewood (left) and Joy Torrez (right).

Camp Family Gathering, 1984.

PART II

Becoming

Whole

Again

The Healing Power of Others

At some time in life we all encounter sorrow. The cycle of life and death is a part of living. Death eventually touches everyone. All, in time, will need comfort. God did not promise a life free from sorrow. That life He reserved for the other side. "And God shall wipe away all tears from their eyes; and there shall be no more death, neither sorrow, nor crying, neither shall there be any more pain" (Revelation 21:4). What He did promise was to be with us through the sorrows of life: "I will never leave thee, nor forsake thee" (Hebrews 13:5).

When death comes, how do we comfort those who grieve? What do we say? What do we do?

Many people are immobilized out of fear that they will do or say the wrong thing. There is no one dramatic gesture that will dissolve the heartache, but there are many acts of thoughtfulness that can convey our concern.

• *Be There* •

What does it mean to care? The persons who mean the most to us are those who, instead of giving advice or solutions, have chosen rather to share our pain and touch our wounds with a gentle and tender hand. The friends who can be silent with us in a moment of despair or confusion, who can stay with us during grief and bereavement, who can face with us the reality of our powerlessness—those are friends who care. Their presence is a healing presence because they accept us on our terms.

The greatest display of love, compassion, and caring shown me at the time of my husband's death was from my church family, some of whom stayed with me for more than eight hours during my terrible ordeal at the hospital. I do not remember their words of comfort, but I do remember their comforting presence.

Cecil was a respected businessman in our city; nevertheless, I was taken completely by surprise at the more than six hundred names that appeared on his funeral register. Of course, not all attended the funeral. Some paid their respects at the funeral home, and some came to the house. Even so, I was overwhelmed at the response of caring people.

Being there is important to those who grieve.

• *Listen* •

True listening in our present-day society has almost become a lost art. The probable cause is that listening requires effort. It involves our total being, not just our ears but our mind, will power, and emotions. Genuine listening involves caring about the other person—caring enough to discern his very heartbeat, caring enough to gently probe until we uncover his innermost feelings. Do we listen—not only with our ears but with our hearts?

Grieving people need to talk about the sudden vacuum in their lives. The best way to get them to open up is with a question: "Would you like to talk about it?" Or later, "How are you adjusting? Life must be hard by yourself; would you like to talk?" The right caring questions will sometimes open a floodgate that acts as a cleansing agent.

Listening also involves knowing what not to say. It is best not to make comments such as:

1. "Don't question God's purpose." (We do question God's purpose.)
2. "It's better now because he (or she) is at peace." (Better for whom? Not me!)
3. "You'll get over this." (How do you know?)
4. "Time heals all wounds." ("All" is an absolute! Some maybe, but not "all.") Time, indeed, does heal, but a grieving person cannot see that far into the future. At the time of initial grief he needs something to relieve the pain of now, not a vague promise of relief in the unknown future.
5. "I know how you feel." Never say this unless you really have gone through the same experience.
6. And never quote Romans 8:28 ("All things work together for good to them that love God") although that verse is eventually a comfort when the grieving process is finished and the reality of the loss accepted. According to my own experience, in the beginning of grief it is wise to avoid saying it. When someone quoted it to me

in the beginning of grief, I can remember thinking, irrationally perhaps, This is not good, and
we both loved God!

7. "Life must go on." (Why?)
8. "You have to be brave." (I'm not brave!)
9. "I have a friend who's going through the same
   thing—it's terrible for her." (How did she get
   into my grief? This is terrible for me!)
10. "I feel almost worse than you do about this."
    (How could you?)
11. If it is a child who has died, never say, "You're
    young; you can have other children." Parents of
    a child who dies do not see it this way. They
    want this child, not other children.
12. If it was a miscarriage, never say, "At least you
    didn't become attached to the child. You don't
    have any memories to mourn." Couples losing
    a child through miscarriage go through grief
    too. Just because the child did not develop to
    maturity does not mean it was not loved. A psy-
    chological attachment has been formed; thus
    the emptiness, void, and grief are real.

To try to soften the pain of death by these well-intentioned but hurtful phrases will make the grieving person
feel all alone and misunderstood in his pain. The caring
words "I'm sorry" minister best to a hurting heart.

• *Send a Note* •

Some of my most treasured notes from friends are simply an expression of how much my loved one meant to
them. It is comforting to know that your loved one meant

something to someone else, too. Each note I received meant something in the healing process of my life. Notes can include personal memories, a shared remembrance of happy times, or a simple "I'm thinking about you."

After a few weeks or months, it is appropriate to send another note or card to let the person know you are still thinking about him. During my five years of widowhood, I received a note or card from my pastor and his wife every few months telling me they cared.

Notes or cards sent on holidays, birthdays, or even Valentine's Day are appreciated. Valentine's Day was especially hard for me. I managed to make it through birthdays, anniversaries, and Christmas but broke down on Valentine's Day.

• *Send Flowers* •

Flowers are a beautiful expression of care and concern, but not everyone can afford flowers. The many floral tributes at Cecil's funeral helped to soothe my hurting heart.

• *Send Small Gifts* •

An appropriate book means a lot to a person in grief. A book of poems or a simple clipping of a poem cut from a magazine is always welcome.

The following poem, "God's Lent Child," by an unknown author, is an example of a small gift that uplifts. My son and daughter-in-law, Steve and Pam Camp, received this poem from one of their friends when their baby, Ashley, died. It helped them to cope. They still did not understand God's ways, but they could understand His love. They had the poem framed in a memory box along with a pair of Baby Ashley's shoes, and today it occupies a prominent place on their memory wall.

• *God's Lent Child* •
(Author Unknown)

"I'll lend you for a little while, a child of mine," God said. "For you to love while he lives, and mourn for when he's dead.

"It may be six or seven months or forty-two or three, but will you, till I call him back, take care of him for Me?

"He'll bring his charms to gladden you, and should his stay be brief, you'll have his lovely memories as solace for your grief.

"I cannot promise he will stay, since ALL from earth return, but there are lessons taught below, I want this child to learn.

"I've looked the whole world over in search for teachers true, and from all those who crowd life's lane, I have chosen you.

"Now will you give him all your love, nor think the labor vain, nor hate Me when I come to take this LENT child back again?"

I fancied that I heard them say, "Dear Lord, Thy will be done. For all the joys THY child will bring, the risk of grief we'll run.

"We'll shelter him with tenderness, we'll love him while we may; and for the happiness we've known, forever grateful stay.

"But should Thy angels call for him much sooner than we've planned, we'll brave the bitter grief that comes and try to understand."

Memorial gifts are another beautiful expression of caring. Among the many memorials I received to various charities, such as the Heart Fund and the Cancer Fund, I also received two living memorials. I received a note stating that a tree had been planted in a national forest as a living memorial. I also received word from the pastor of a faraway church that a tree was being planted in the churchyard as a living memorial to Cecil. Knowing that life will exist in the presence of death is a comforting gift.

A lasting tribute to Cecil's memory were bookmarks I received from a friend that were made from the newspaper account of his obituary.

All of these are certainly caring expressions from caring people.

• *Extend an Invitation* •

Invite the person for coffee, for shopping, or for lunch. People in grief often accept invitations but cancel at the last minute. Fearing they will break down in public causes many such cancellations. Gentle encouragement can help turn futility and despair into hope for a better tomorrow. Walking with someone, rather than merely showing him the way, is the essence of caring.

• *Don't Scald Their Feet* •

What does scalding feet have to do with ministering to the needs of others? In the account of Jesus' washing the disciples' feet (John 13:4-17), Jesus set an example in ministering to others that we should attempt to follow:

1. *First,* Jesus' act was unannounced. He simply got up silently from the meal, poured a basin of water, draped a

towel around His waist, and began to wash their feet. The scribes and Pharisees did their good deeds and then announced them for all to hear, but Jesus did not go out and announce, "Look what I did. I washed My disciples' feet." No, He simply did it. He gave us an example to follow. When we minister to others, let us do it unannounced.

In December 1982 my husband, Cecil, was scheduled for open-heart surgery in Houston, Texas. Before our departure for Houston, one of the men of the church slipped a fifty-dollar bill into Cecil's coat pocket without saying a word. He did not announce it for others to hear or even for us to hear; he simply did it. Sensing a need, he responded to it unannounced.

2. *Second,* ministering to others includes receiving as well as giving. When it came Peter's turn, he said, "No, Lord, You're not going to wash my feet!" But Jesus said, "If you're going to be useful to Me, Peter, I must wash your feet."

Pride sometimes gets in our way of receiving, as it did with Peter. When we are down, it is hard to admit that we need others. We put on our "all's well" face when deep inside we are hurting. Pride keeps others at arm's length. The incident of the fifty dollars, pride tried to refuse the gift. Pride did not want to admit it was needed.

3. *Third,* before God can use us to minister to others, we ourselves must become vulnerable. It is difficult to admit we need help. The beautiful thing about Peter is that when he responded to Jesus, he made a complete about-face: "Not just my feet, Lord, but my hands and head. Wash me all over!" Peter rid himself of his pride, became vulnerable, and admitted his need. When we accepted the gift of fifty dollars, we became vulnerable and admitted our need.

4. *Last,* when we wash feet, figuratively speaking, we must be careful about the temperature of the water. We should not bring a pail of boiling water and say, "Stick them in here." Feet need to be washed gently, not scalded. It is possible to "minister" to someone in such an offensive and harsh manner that we do more harm than good. (Remember the well-intentioned but hurtful phrases listed before?)

The man who gave us the fifty dollars could have said, "I know you're down and out; here's fifty dollars." Or, "My wife won't like this, but here's fifty dollars." Or, "I should be paying a bill with this, but here's fifty dollars." Or, he could have made sure others saw him give the gift, or bragged about it afterwards. In so doing, he would have been scalding our feet.

When ministering to others, gentle encouragement is what is needed. "How are you adjusting? Would you like to talk? Let's get a cup of coffee (or lunch or dinner). Let's go shopping together (or fishing or walking). I want to be your friend."

Let's not scald their feet.

The Healing Power of Hope

To become whole again is the cry of every grieving person. To be a "half person" is having part of ourselves wrenched and torn away. To become whole again, however, is an active pursuit, not a passive one. We must actively search for wholeness. Searching implies keeping on the move, actively reaching, actively seeking.

The signs of a whole person are these: being thankful for life rather than bitter for what life brings, being eager to give and also willing to receive, giving wholehearted effort to each undertaking, knowing that life is too short to spend being unhappy, realizing that problems of life either disappear or solutions are found, and changing problems of life into challenges and opportunities.

To become a truly whole person again requires the peace of God. We desperately want peace, but where do we find personal peace? Peace is not passive. We must pursue it (I Peter 3:11). We must look for it and track it down. Peace does not just happen. It is made, built, and constructed.

The world offers peace through sedatives and tranquilizers, but not a permanent peace. "We have peace with God through our Lord Jesus Christ" (Romans 5:1). Jesus' peace is not like any peace the world gives. His is uninterrupted, not occasional, and takes us safely through the storms of life.

In order to find the peace that only God can give, we must, first of all, be aware that God speaks to us through the circumstances of life. When God speaks through circumstances, such circumstances take on many forms. Sometimes it is through financial collapse. Sometimes it is an illness. Sometimes it is a disappointment. Sometimes it is a tragedy. God uses all circumstances in life to speak to us. What we hear through these circumstances is affected not only by our relationship with Him but also by another factor: our understanding of who He is. We need to ponder questions such as these:

- What is our understanding of God? Of His character?
- Do we view Him as a loving or demanding father?
- As a patient or intolerant teacher?
- As an understanding or insensitive counselor?
- As a generous or reluctant provider?
- As a faithful or inconsistent sustainer?
- As an intimate or distant friend?
- As a gentle or unwilling healer?

We must understand the character of the God we serve before we can really hear Him speak through the circumstances of our lives. If we do not understand His character, we see only the circumstance and not the God who allowed the circumstance. Only by knowing the God of the circumstance will we find the peace He offers.

When we understand God's character, we see things

from a different perspective. The things that worry us lose their grip. The things that weaken us, God turns into strength. Our inward look at problems or situations is replaced by a heavenly view. We see them from God's viewpoint.

Seeing from God's viewpoint brings hope, and hope is the trailblazer that brings the peace of God. What is hope?

* Hope expects the coming of something new.
* Hope looks ahead toward what is not yet.
* Hope accepts and risks.
* Hope keeps on going even when something does not work out the first time.
* Hope goes fearlessly into things without knowing how they will turn out.
* Hope dares to stay open to whatever today may offer.

God wants us to be happy, motivated, and excited about life. There is excitement in hope. Hope is a God-given sense of expectancy, an inner peace that cannot be swayed by the circumstances of the moment. Hope is always expecting something good from God.

* Develop Hope Not Hopelessness *

No matter how hard life's blows, people who have hope for tomorrow manage to come through smiling. The secret is to choose a positive perspective. Instead of dwelling on what we have lost, we should consider what we have left. When we begin to count our blessings, many more will surface: beautiful memories of the past, blessings of the present, and hopes for the future.

Hope is an amazing thing. Doctors respect it as a powerful medicine. Surgeons are wary of operating on people who lack it. It has been proven that patients facing surgery have a better chance of surviving if they have a positive outlook, one with hope for tomorrow. Those with no hope have no will to live, thereby lessening their chances of survival.

News stories relate how social workers deal with starving children of war-torn countries when they are finally rescued. They place a piece of bread in the child's hand when they put him to bed at night. Clutching that piece of bread and knowing he has food to eat tomorrow brings hope, calms the child, and helps him sleep.

Yes, hope is an amazing thing. Romans 4:18 speaks of hoping against hope. That is hoping against all odds. Even though we can see no hope, we hope anyway. Hoping against hope for good to come out of our experience, God will bring it to pass.

Develop hope, not hopelessness.

• *Don't Wallow in Self-Pity* •

I have heard it said, "We shouldn't wallow in self-pity, but sometimes it's okay to swish our feet a little." In other words, everyone can use some "feel bad" time before moving on. "Feel bad" time, however, is not a comfortable place in which to live.

We must begin to find ways to fill up the emptiness caused by our loss. Filling up the emptiness fosters hope for tomorrow. Becoming more involved in church, in our community, and with others is a beginning place to fill up the emptiness.

Having suffered loss, we have passed through an experience whereby we can reach out and minister to others. If we wallow in self-pity, however, and let that experience isolate us from others so that we grow indifferent to their hurts, we have done God an injustice. By reaching out to help others, we foster hope for ourselves.

• *Learn to Laugh* •

It helps if we try to see the funny side of tough days. My brother, Travis, has the unique ability of seeing something funny in every incident of life. Like the rest of us, he must have bad days, but on the whole, life to him is funny.

Pull out your favorite cartoons and joke books. Try to incorporate fun activities into your day. Fun and pleasure relax tension and help us to laugh.

Laughter is a tonic that makes today better and raises hopes for tomorrow. Laughter counters isolation and puts people in touch with others.

One psychologist encourages cancer patients to tell their favorite funny stories to each other. "It elevates their mood and helps in pain control," he says.

If laughter helps in physical pain control, it also helps in emotional pain control. Those in grief feel guilty the first time they experience pleasure and laughter. Because of the death of a loved one, they feel that they, too, should be dead to feelings and emotions equated with life.

Laughter can erase humiliation and embarrassment. Some of the funniest things we laugh at today were once humiliating and embarrassing episodes of the past. When we take these out of the closet and share them, they become hilarious events.

One such embarrassing event that spawns laughter in my family whenever it is mentioned is this one:

Stepping from my kitchen into the garage one morning, I accidentally locked myself out of the house. Clad only in a filmy nightgown, I shrank from the idea of seeking help from the neighbors.

Forced to stay confined to the garage from eight in the morning until my husband's return from work at half past six that evening, I spent the day in hysterical tears. When Cecil returned home and found me in the garage still in my nightgown, he said, "Why aren't you dressed? We're supposed to be at the church in thirty minutes." More hysterical tears!

Still humiliated by my ordeal, I was further mortified to learn that news travels as though it has wings. At church, my pastor quipped from the pulpit about my day of "prayer and fasting."

When my brother, Travis, broke his foot, he was rushed to the hospital emergency room where his wife, Patricia, a registered nurse, was on duty. Seeing Travis's predicament, Patricia burst into hysterical laughter. This shocked the doctors and nurses standing nearby until they learned that Travis had been conducting a safety meeting for a group of Boy Scouts when a heavy table collapsed during his safety demonstration. His foot was caught underneath and broken when the table came crashing down. The hospital staff immediately dubbed him "Mr. Safety," which has been his name for almost twenty years now.

Recalling embarrassing episodes can get the adrenalin flowing as the healing power of laughter calms a troubled spirit. After a loss, it is all right to live again, to laugh again. Laughter dispels tension and apathy, brushes the cobwebs from our brain, and stimulates the flow of hope.

King Solomon said it best: "A merry heart doeth good like a medicine" (Proverbs 17:22).

• *Borrow Hope from Others* •

The success of Alcoholics Anonymous and similar support groups is based on a simple formula: "I've made it, and with my help, so can you." The formula works because hope is contagious. It is hard to continue feeling despondent about your husband losing his job when you talk to a friend who has had the same experience. Often you can fan the spark of hope by talking to a friend or neighbor who knows what it is like to live with wayward children, to live through divorce, or to experience the death of a loved one.

Relatives, friends, and neighbors who can offer advice and moral support are a definite asset. There is no more effective way to relieve emotional pain than to be in contact with another human being who understands what you are going through.

So, if you cannot muster up enough hope for yourself, borrow it from others. It works!

◦ *Know That You Still Have a Purpose* ◦

Sometimes people lose respect for themselves when they feel they have lost their reason for living. A purpose in life keeps us going. It will put us back on our feet when we have been knocked down. When we dwell on events of the past, most often we never are able to recapture the high purpose of living.

After Cecil's death, I often cried to God to please take me home, too. As time passed, however, I began to see that there were things still left for me to do. God must have felt that I was still needed, or most assuredly, He would have taken me, too.

Feeling that God could see purpose in my life caused me eventually to feel it, too. When my dad was first confined to a nursing home in 1989 after having been hospitalized for a long period of time, I sensed a new purpose in my life. Getting up at 5:00 AM and going to the nursing home before going to work, I fulfilled that purpose by making sure Dad ate his breakfast and getting him settled for the day. Reaching out to others brings a purpose to living.

Each day I live, I know there is a purpose for that day. Some days I find the purpose in tasks of solitude, other days in being with people. Whatever the day brings, knowing that I still have a purpose brings hope for a better tomorrow.

◦ *Don't Panic When Things Seem Hopeless* ◦

Admittedly, we are perplexed by life. We have prayed for health, and sickness has come; we have prayed for loved ones to get well, and they have died; we have prayed for material blessings, but they did not come. When things seem hopeless, that is when we need more than ever to have hope.

It is not easy to relax in a crisis, but the chances of survival are much better for those who dare to hope. Even a tiny whisper of hope can set us spinning in a positive direction with the expectation that tomorrow will be better than today.

Hope sustains us through adversity. Let us ignite that spark of hope!

◦ *Hope in the Form of an Ordinary-Looking Toy* ◦

It was just an ordinary-looking toy. It had no distinguishing marks; it looked like any one of a million others sold at toy counters across the country. Yet this particular little varmint led an existence quite unlike any of its counterparts. I heard the incredible story of hope and the little rubber snake for the first time last year when I attended the wedding of my niece, Angela.

My car was packed, really packed. I squeezed into the driver's side of the little Nissan as Mother squeezed into the passenger's side. My daughter-in-law, Pam Camp, rearranged the boxes in the back seat to give herself a little leg room. The three of us were on our way to Johnson City, Tennessee, to attend the wedding.

Clothes for three women, including clothes for a wedding and wedding functions, had been a challenge to the expertise of my son, Steve, who was packing the car. As he stuffed in the last bag and slammed the trunk, he groaned, "Surely there's nothing left in your closets," which were my brother's identical words when we arrived in Johnson City two days later after our nine-hundred-mile trip from Texas.

The garden wedding was held on the spacious grounds of a beautiful old mansion in this East Tennessee town situated at the foothills of the picturesque Appalachian Mountains. The late October sunlight played hide-and-seek with fluffy, white, low-hanging clouds. I watched as my brother, Travis, proudly escorted his only daughter down the flower-strewn garden path.

"Her mother and I," was his sober response to the minister's time-honored question of who gives this woman to be married. As he gently handed Angela to her waiting bridegroom and took his place beside his wife, Patricia, I could not help but notice Patricia's composure suddenly crumble.

Attributing the tears to the sentimental nature of the occasion, I dismissed them until sometime later when I heard for the first time the fascinating story of the little rubber snake. It was a story of hope, encouragement, and love.

Wedding guests gone, the family was gathered together. Passing my coffee cup for a refill, I innocently remarked that I, too, had cried when my children married.

"Oh, that's not why she was crying." Travis refilled my cup. He began his strange tale by telling us how thirty-five years ago, shortly after their marriage, he slipped a tiny rubber snake into Patricia's handbag.

"Travis Nevels! Why?" Mother nearly choked on her coffee.

"You know your son," Patricia retorted. "Always the clown."

"What happened when you found it?" Demure Pam was wide-eyed.

"What do you think happened?" Travis laughed. "She screamed; then handbag, contents, and snake went flying through the air."

"Then what?" I, too, was fascinated. I knew my brother was a prankster, but to his new bride?

"Naturally, I was angry and upset and had reacted exactly as was expected of me," Patricia said. Glancing at Travis, she added, "He then had the nerve to say that he had put it there as a gesture of love and to show me he wanted to share his life with me. Quick thinking!"

"What happened to it? Did you throw it away?" Pam shuddered and made a face.

"No, as a matter of fact, I didn't," Patricia said. "Several days later I decided to get even, so I packed the despicable little creature in Travis's lunch box and secretly gloated as I imagined his embarrassment when he opened the box in front of his friends. But a strange thing happened. Travis never mentioned the incident to me. I forgot about the toy snake until some months later when, at a low point in my life, it mysteriously appeared, tucked in a corner of my lingerie drawer."

Travis again took up the tale. "Some time after that, when I, too, needed cheering up, I found him stuffed in the pocket of my coat."

As the story unfolded, we learned that when spirits were low the little critter would automatically turn up tucked in a shoe, a pocket, a briefcase, or a purse. Through the years, he has made untimely appearances at graduations and births, slipped into hospital rooms and church services, turned up on family vacations and second honeymoons, and silently stood vigil during illnesses and deaths. His message of hope and encouragement was there for Travis during our dad's battle with Alzheimer's disease, was there for Patricia during her father's terminal illness and death, was there for both of them at the death of their baby grandson, and is standing by now with both of them during her brother's battle with leukemia.

What preserved the allurement of his appearances? No doubt, the fact that no one but the two of them knew of his existence. Elusively he drifted in and out of their lives with his mysterious comings and goings. Even so, months and sometimes years would elapse before he would make one of his unannounced appearances. Then, when he was seemingly forgotten, the little scamp would put in his magical appearance with his silent message of cheer seeming to say, I love you and want to share your life.

Wiping a tear, Patricia finished the story by telling us that when Travis handed Angela to her waiting bridegroom and took his place beside her, his wife, he gently slipped the tiny creature into her hand.

Where is the little rascal today?

I do not know, but I am convinced that when there is another need, the little critter (now thirty-five years old) will make his appearance with his silent testimony of hope, encouragement, and love.

The Healing Power of God's Word

In the midst of grief, too often we think we are trusting when we are merely controlling our panic. True faith in God gives not only a calm exterior but a quiet heart.

By studying God's creation, we understand better how He shapes our individual lives. Jesus taught by parable, comparing the natural with the spiritual. The following illustrations from nature communicate that God cares for us, that He has a plan for our individual lives, and that if we will allow Him, He will work in us and through us His perfect plan. Through His Word He can instill in us a quiet heart.

• *The Vine* •

I am the vine, ye are the branches. . . . If a man abide not in me, he is . . . withered (John 15:5-6).

I was very proud of my morning glory vines. The little fence of chicken wire my husband had erected for them to run on seemed sturdy enough. The sumptuous blue blossoms were a beauty to behold as each morning I carefully tended them while noting their prolific growth. Soon the chicken wire was completely covered with dark green leaves and tiny blue blossoms.

One morning we were startled by a commotion on the patio. As we dashed out to investigate, the neighbor's dog, Ted, was standing nearby wagging his tail. I was horror struck as my gaze focused on the gaping hole in the chicken wire!

We surmised that Ted had been playfully chasing something in our yard, which was his custom, and had run through the fence.

"Your morning glories are not hurt, hon," my husband, Cecil, assured me as he repaired the hole in the chicken wire. And, sure enough, they were still standing, radiating dark green foliage and munificent blue blossoms. My pet flowers had not been harmed.

Time reveals all things, however, as I discovered a few mornings later. The green leaves and the blue flowers that had deceived us a few days before were now wilted and dead. Upon close examination, we discovered that only the vine was still living, because its roots ran deep into the ground. What we had not noticed earlier was that the branches had been partially severed from the vine. This was not noticeable except by careful, close scrutiny.

As I stood there bemoaning the fate of my beloved morning glories, Jesus' words leaped to mind: "I am the vine, ye are the branches. . . . If a man abide not in me, he . . . is withered."

As long as I am attached to the Lord (the Vine), my life will flourish and grow and be a joy for others to behold. If I become separated from Him, by disobedience to His Word, others may not even know at first. There may not be a noticeable change—I will look the same and act the same for a while—but time will tell. The branch cannot live of itself—it must be attached to the vine! Help me, Lord, I pray, to remain attached to You so that others may be blessed through my life.

Ten years have passed since the incident of the morning glories. Many dark valleys, including the struggles of widowhood, have tried to sever this "branch" from its vine, but I have found that the Lord is faithful to tenderly protect a bruised reed.

• *The Clay* •

O LORD, thou art our father; we are the clay, and thou our potter; and we all are the work of thy hand (Isaiah 64:8).

Then I went down to the potter's house, and, behold, he wrought a work on the wheels. . . . Then the word of the LORD came to me, saying, . . . Behold, as the clay is in the potter's hand, so are ye in mine hand (Jeremiah 18:3-6).

Pottery making is one of the oldest of human crafts. One of the first inventions of man was the potter's wheel.

When clay is first dug from the earth it is not pure but is mixed with sand, small stones, pebbles, and dried leaves. The potter must remove all grit, pebbles, and other substances so that the clay will be perfectly smooth. Ancient potters learned to accomplish this by mixing water with the clay and letting the mixture stand in a large basin. Impurities fall to the bottom while the upper layer of clay and water is pumped into an adjoining basin. This process is repeated several times in order to make sure that all impurities have been removed.

When the living water of God's Spirit first washes our lives, oh, how clean we feel! Old things pass away, and behold all things become new! We are born anew! Cleansed!

As time passes, subsequent washings of the Spirit bring us a little closer to being the vessel God has pictured us to be. The Almighty must sift us many times in order to remove those things that cling to us when we have been dug from the earth. God begins the process of removing the sand and the stones from our life. Bitterness, resentment, and ill feelings must be washed away many times by His living water.

The potter then takes the clay in his hands and squeezes, rolls, and kneads it to remove all air bubbles and to get the proper consistency. Sometimes we do not understand the workings of God in our lives. As He rolls and kneads, we do not realize that if the air bubbles are not squeezed there can be no finished product. We fail to see the end result—only the pressures of the moment.

When the clay is of the proper consistency, the potter throws a lump onto the center of the rotating disk of the potter's wheel. Plunging both thumbs in the center of the clay mass, he begins to fashion the vessel. When he has formed the desired shape, the potter sets the vessel aside to dry and harden.

It is interesting that the potter does not work on his clay every day, but as he wishes. Sometimes we, as the clay, become disgruntled if we cannot feel God moving and blessing in our lives. Where is God? Has He forgotten where we live? Perhaps He has just set us aside to harden.

When dried, the vessel is centered upside down on the wheel. (Uh-oh, my world has turned upside down again!)

As the wheel rotates, tools made of bone or wood are used to refine the vessel by shaving off unwanted clay. (Oh, how that hurts!)

After this, the vessel is ready to be fired. The potter always puts his vessels through the fire twice. The first firing hardens the clay so that it will not crumble. The second firing is for beauty and permanency. We would most certainly like to skip the fire, but God in His wisdom does not want us to crumble. It is also His will for the beauty of the Christian life to be permanent, not temporary.

Even though a skillful potter can shape a vessel into any desired shape, if the clay reacts adversely to the potter's touch, the vessel is marred. The potter may then attempt to rework the clay—a touch more water, a piece of grit removed, knead and roll. Sometimes he succeeds, but at other times the vessel becomes brittle and hard and breaks in the potter's hand. Then he has no other choice but to toss it aside with the rejects in the potter's field.

It is strange to note that the vessel breaks while it is in the potter's hand. We may be in our Potter's hands, but are we flexible and pliable in His hands? Do we resent the Potter shaping our lives? When struggles, griefs, and trials come along, do we resist His molding? If so, we will become hard and brittle, eventually breaking under His touch. Oh, how terrible it would be to one day find oneself among the rejects in the potter's field!

• *The Snow* •

Though your sins be as scarlet, they shall be as white as snow (Isaiah 1:18).

Snow! Mr. Webster defines this powdery stuff as "water

vapor frozen into crystals that fall to earth in soft, white flakes and spread upon it as a white layer."

There are many people in our world who have never seen snow because it falls on only about one-third of the earth's surface. They have not experienced the purity, the whiteness, the gentleness of this element called snow. Yet, in some parts of the world, such as the Arctic regions, people are susceptible to snow blindness. Large snowy areas reflect a great amount of dazzling light, and snow blindness will occur if the eyes are not protected from the glare of the sun reflecting on the snow. When snow blindness occurs, a person is temporarily blinded and will see red. The Eskimos who live in snowy regions wear sun shields made of bone that sit in front of the eyes like goggles.

As a child, I remember wishing for snow, deep snow. A snowfall in our part of the country, however, usually meant light flurries, and some years even flurries were nonexistent. Childhood is gone now, but recently those long-ago childish wishes became reality.

One bleak, cold morning last winter I awoke to an unexpected, unaccustomed eight-inch snowfall. Silently, undetected, it had fallen. The possibility of snow had not been in the weather forecast. But, suddenly—eight inches deep! It was a most unusual sight for this East Texas girl!

As I looked across our backyard and into the woods beyond, my mind was captivated by the picture of perfection. Why, only the day before I had gazed at that same scene and my thoughts had been, How barren, how bleak, how ugly. But now, the Master Painter had opened the windows of heaven and dipped His brush in "angel mist." Ugliness was swallowed up in beauty! Imperfection was wrapped in perfection!

The dead, ugly grass of the day before lay invisible under its sparkling, dazzling blanket of pure, white, driven snow. Where did all the imperfections go? No longer were they visible. Where was that hole the dogs had dug? It was no longer there. The ugly red clay and rock patch where no grass will grow lay quietly unseen under the shelter of its fluffy new blanket. The stark, barren trees were now standing resplendent with their branches radiating God's outpouring.

As I viewed this unexpected, awesome scene, a verse of Scripture, as gentle as the fallen snow, floated through my head: "Though your sins be as scarlet, they shall be as white as snow." The scene that I beheld with my natural eye is also the scene that takes place in a person's spiritual life when the blood of Jesus Christ washes away the ugliness of sin and provides a beautiful, covering blanket of white, pure righteousness. Just as Adam and Eve wore the covering of the coats of skins provided by God, we wear the covering provided by God—Jesus Christ. His precious blood creates the beautiful, pure, white blanket. His righteousness will sparkle and shine like a beacon light in our lives causing others to behold the purity of our covering. Our imperfections are hidden in Him! "Your life is hid with Christ in God" (Colossians 3:3).

Just as there are many people in this world who have never seen snow, there are many who have never experienced for themselves the covering of the righteousness of Christ. Our lives, as children of God, may be the only Bible some will ever read. We may be the only spiritual example some will ever know. What a challenge and what a responsibility!

When people come in contact with us, do they see the

purity and the freshness of our covering? Do they get snow blindness from observing our life? Do they see red as a result of snow blindness—the redness of the blood of Jesus? Oh, that they would have to wear goggles as the brilliance of His righteousness blinds them.

Let all of us purpose with a greater fervency to stay covered with the precious blood of Christ so that this world can behold and also know the One who said, "Though your sins be as scarlet, they shall be as white as snow."

• *The Rose* •

The desert shall rejoice, and blossom as the rose (Isaiah 35:1).

The rose has been special to humanity from the earliest history. It is the eternal flower of love, the emblem of sentiment. It has become a symbol of fragrance and beauty; no other flower has had so many poetic tributes paid it.

In literature and poetry, the rose has stood as a symbol of purity and innocence. In art, the rose has become a symbol of beauty and peace. In horticulture, the rose stands for permanency. It endures from year to year, blooming each season, attaining growth.

It is not extraordinary, then, that the rose should have the universal place it holds in the hearts of people of all classes and locales. It is the universal flower.

It is not surprising that one of the titles attributed to Jesus is the "Rose of Sharon." "I am the rose of Sharon, and the lily of the valleys" (Song of Solomon 2:1).

A dedicated Christian life is, like the rose, a symbol of beauty, peace, purity, and innocence. It permeates the atmosphere with the sweet-smelling fragrance of God's Spirit.

There is an essence in what we are that transcends all we say or do. Some personalities are fragrant; some are not. Some leave a beauty behind them that lingers like perfume; others leave only disappointment. Is it any wonder, then, that a dedicated Christian life is a constant, unspoken testimony to the saving and satisfying power of the Lord Jesus Christ?

Like the rose, a consecrated life endures from year to year under every circumstance of life, blooming in its season, attaining Christian growth, and emitting a sense of permanency to the beholder.

Weeds need no cultivation. They seem to thrive on neglect. Contrarily, roses must be cultivated. They must be pruned, dug around, and watered in order to produce healthy, beautiful blossoms free from disease and fungus.

Likewise, the Christian life must be pruned, dug around, and watered by God in order to produce a life free from the disease of sin and the fungus of worldliness.

Oil extracted from the petal of the rose is used in perfume making. Perfumers must press and crush the delicate petals in order to extract the fragrant oil.

Similarly, so that others may benefit from the fragrant aroma of a Christian life, the dedicated child of God must sometimes endure pressure, heartaches, crushing blows. But when they are finished, the sweet perfume titillating the senses of all who behold is a multiplied blessing to many and a provoking testimony to the glory of the Rose of Sharon.

Standing at attention, ever present as sentinels and guards amid the beautiful roses, are the thorns. The purpose of these drawn bayonets is to protect the delicate flower from enemies who would destroy it.

God's Spirit living within is our sentinel, our drawn bayonet, to protect the beauty of the Christian life. If we will heed the pricks of this sustainer of life, all enemies that threaten to destroy will, in turn, be destroyed.

If we will but yield to the life-protecting piercings of the Spirit, all attitudes of self-pity, doubt, and hopelessness must flee! Saul of Tarsus heeded the Lord's warning: "It is hard for thee to kick against the pricks" (Acts 9:5). Saul fell to the ground. So great was his encounter with God that day on the road to Damascus that nothing was able to deter him. The goading of God's Spirit turned that persecutor of Christians, Saul of Tarsus, into the mighty apostle Paul, the greatest witness Christianity has ever known.

We, too, can have fullness of life and be the person God intended for us to be if we will rely not on our human power or human strength, but on God's power—the Spirit within leading and guiding.

• *The Gold* •

When he hath tried me, I shall come forth as gold (Job 23:10).

Gold is of no value unrefined. Gold ore is not useful. It is in a dormant stage—dull, unattractive, and useless. Moreover, gold ore cannot be shaped and molded into anything of beauty until it is first subjected to the heat of a white-hot furnace. As the gold ore begins to liquify, all the impurities rise to the top and can be skimmed off, leaving only the pure, beautiful, shimmering metal that can then be shaped and molded into a work of art, very valuable and very beautiful.

God has always tried His people in the furnace of

affliction. It is in the heat of the furnace that the dross separates from the true gold of the Christian character.

Through the heat of the furnace in the afflictions of life, God shows us our weaknesses and impurities and teaches us to lean on Him. He permits the trials of life not only to strengthen and purify our own lives but so that through our reaction and example, others might be blessed. Whether we want to admit it or not, our actions and reactions affect others. "None of us liveth to himself" (Romans 14:7).

What is our reaction when things go wrong? Do we become bitter and blame God, or do adverse circumstances draw us closer to Him? The way we conduct our lives leaves a lasting impression for good or for bad on someone else.

It is a sobering thought to know that my life makes a difference in the lives of others. Can they see Jesus in me? Am I making a difference in my world for good? Am I making a difference by emanating the purity of the Lord Jesus Christ? Can others see godly qualities radiating from my life? Can they feel the love and mercy of God flowing through me and touching them? To know that God is real, the world must see Him at work in my life.

Nothing in life is unforeseen by God. God has allowed the struggles of life. Do we thank Him for His care through the struggles? Are we thankful, or are we busy in second guessing? "If only I had done this or that or somebody had not done this or that, or if that had not happened—my whole life would have been different." We may find ourselves fighting against God if we fail to realize that He has had His hand in all our past.

Paul the apostle recognized the hand of God in his life.

He knew that his life had not developed by accident, and that God had been working out His purposes. Paul acted when he could to change adverse situations in which he found himself, but when he could not change them, he accepted them. We should do the same. "I have learned in whatsoever state I am, therewith to be content" (Philippians 4:11).

The Healing Power of Time

Although overwhelming sorrow can temporarily dis-organize our lives, it is not an insoluble problem. Many of us, when we suffer deeply, may think we are over-whelmed and cannot cope; however, as time passes, life carries us with it and we rally and find happiness. It is sur-prising how, even after much sorrow, we can be happy again as time passes.

There is healing power in time. Time raises hopes for a better tomorrow. The important thing is to give ourselves time.

Time alone, however, will heal nothing if a person does not go through active grief. Grief itself takes time, and once that time has elapsed, the raw edges of suffering will begin to fade and healing will come.

During grief, the roller coaster effect is very much evi-dent. We have lost control of our life. Others seem to be in control, not we ourselves. We feel trapped in situations of life. In order to gain control of our lives once again, we must first face the fact that it is out of control and then seek ways to get ourselves back in control. Assuredly, the greatest accomplishment in life is the mastery of oneself. The realization that we are improving our lives brings self-confidence and happiness.

During grief, sometimes we fail to gain control of our lives simply because we never attempt anything that is difficult. We take the easy road; we sit back and let time slip away. The mere passage of time does not bring healing, however. It is only time lived to the fullest that brings complete healing.

To gain control of our lives means the forming of new habits. Certain steps are involved in the forming of any new habits:

1. *First,* we must be convinced in our own mind that we want to gain mastery over our life. To be convinced means no wavering, no indecisiveness.

2. *Next,* we must begin. Many good habits are never formed simply because we put off beginning. The longer the interval between the time we decide to do something about our lives and the time we actually begin, the greater the difficulty we face. There is power in making a decision and then beginning to do something about it.

3. Once we begin, we must keep going. We must not be satisfied until we are in complete control again. When defeats come, and they will, picking ourselves up and beginning again will bring victory.

4. Once we have formed right habits life begins to

take on a new balance, an internal equilibrium. The satisfaction of accomplishment gives strength and stability that we have never realized before.

The following suggestions will help us to begin to take control of our lives.

• *Take One Day at a Time* •

Running from problems instead of facing them delays the grieving process. Taking each day as it comes sounds too easy, but a grieving person cannot cope with more than this day's problems. When we start thinking about endless days with these same kinds of problems, we become overwhelmed. Solving one day's problems at a time, however, will give us a small portion of satisfaction. It helps us to feel that we are getting our lives back together.

A good strategy here is to have a definite plan for getting through today. Wondering what will happen to our lives five years in the future, one year, one month, or even one week is too overwhelming. We cannot cope.

Often it helps to write things down. Making lists of things to do allows us to identify priorities. Marking off things as we do them is another helpful strategy. It increases our feeling of satisfaction.

At the beginning of each day write down what you plan to accomplish this day:
- *pay bills* (which ones?)
- *write letters* (to whom?)
- *clean house* (which rooms? vacuum? mop? dust?)
- *run errands* (where? grocery? bank? gas station?)

Being specific helps to identify priorities. Having a

written plan and crossing off things as they are done gives a sense of accomplishment. It gives us a sense of well-being, causing us to think, Hey, maybe I can get it together again.

This approach keeps us from being overwhelmed by the overall scope and magnitude of our problems. Breaking things down into segments builds confidence. The question becomes not "How can I get along for the rest of my life?" but "How can I get along this day?" This encourages us to stop worrying and start working.

When Cecil died, I truly felt that I would never come to terms with his death. My life was suddenly so scattered and disorganized that I feared this was to be my lot in life. I learned, however, that fears are vague and shadowy like an object seen in semidarkness. Fears are difficult to defeat because we allow them to remain vague and shadowy. Shadows in a dim light take on grotesque shapes and are not in reality what they appear to be. When we lay our fears out before us in full light, we begin to see them for what they are, not what we have imagined them to be.

As I began examining my fears in the light and started taking each day as it came, one day I discovered that I was coping. I was reorganizing my life.

We may not fully grasp the design of our lives until we learn to move with events as they evolve. Taking each day as it comes and moving with it is the beginning of a new life, one that will eventually give us pleasure because we ourselves were the catalyst.

• *Establish a Routine* •

In order for time to be a healer, we must first establish some kind of order in our chaotic life. There is healing in routine. Routine is to our sanity what a rudder is to a ship: it steers and guides. Without a rudder a ship would drift aimlessly. Likewise, without routine a grieving person will drift aimlessly, with no goal, no aim, and no reason for living.

The widowed person needs a reason to get up in the morning, a reason to stay healthy and neatly groomed. Self-worth often dies with a spouse.

Occupying our time with worthwhile pursuits will hasten healing. Having a job helped me get organized. A job outside the home is therapeutic. When we must get up and be somewhere else at a certain time, our minds are temporarily off ourselves and on other things. For a certain portion of the day, we are forced to put our own personal problems aside.

Even if you do not have an outside job, having specific hours for meals, housework, sleep, and so on, and keeping those hours diligently as if they are appointments, will do much in creating order from a disordered life.

Widows with children still at home seem to bounce back quicker than those who live alone. Being forced to think about the welfare of others forces their minds on problems other than their own. Being compelled to conform to the children's routine of school activities seems to bring a normalcy to life in a shorter period of time.

Occupying oneself with an enjoyable hobby helps the time to pass pleasantly. Grieving people who occupy their time by reading, sewing, cooking, or gardening seem to possess a calmer spirit than those who occupy time by flipping through endless photograph albums reliving the past or sitting for hours staring vacantly into space.

Occupying time through volunteer work (church, hospital, nursing home) is helpful to many. Volunteer work helps us to reach out to the needs of others, thereby ministering to ourselves also. Helping others through their own traumatic times of life hastens the healing process of our own lives.

Idleness causes depression. It is essential to our mental well-being to be pleasantly occupied. We need an organized and structured day so that we can look forward and know how each day will be filled. Thoughts need to be claimed by outside interests so that time seems to pass more quickly. Time hangs heavy when we are idle. We turn thoughts inward when we are idle.

There are many small, happy experiences in everyday life that are waiting to lift our spirits. We do not need some great happiness to bring back joy in living. The little things will do that, as soon as we have eyes to see them.

One widow in our city learned to turn small, everyday experiences into a healer by taking to her kitchen. She bakes bread and cakes for the nursing home and cooks for her Sunday school class. In small groups she has served dinner to many and invited friends for tea and coffee.

Likewise, find something you enjoy, then do it. Take a structured trip with a group; invite friends to your home; spend a day at the library; try your hands at crafts, sewing, or knitting; create your own recipe books; keep a journal. Keeping pleasantly occupied helps time to become a healer.

• *Unlearn Old Habits* •

When someone close to us dies there are daily activities that are permanently altered by the absence of the loved one. As a result, we must unlearn old habits.

When Cecil died it was many months before I could go directly home from work. Going home to an empty house was overwhelming. When I got off work, I would go to the mall and spend the evening hours sitting and idly watching the bustling crowd. I was subconsciously unlearning old habits.

Our special time together had been the evening. By going to the mall at that time I was trying to occupy myself with other activities. It hurt less than spending the time alone at home. Diversion, indeed, supports a flagging spirit. As I unlearned old habits, I gradually learned new habits and, in time, learned to occupy myself with many different things in the evening. Going to the mall and watching people became unnecessary when I found new interests.

During grief, we consider ourselves in a prison of loneliness, but a prison can be transformed. "And at midnight Paul and Silas prayed, and sang praises unto God: and the prisoners heard them" (Acts 16:25). No prison could ever hold Paul's spirit. Much of the New Testament was written from his prison cell. By using our time constructively, we too can transform our prison of loneliness, thereby hastening the healing process.

• *Learn Something New* •

Learning something new is another way to encourage time to become a healer. One of the reasons the days of our youth seem so full and long is that they are days of learning and discovery.

After Cecil's death, I went back to college at night to study creative writing. I can truthfully say these were some of the most rewarding days of my life.

For many of us, learning ends when we leave high school or college as a young person, but this does not have to be. Learning can be a challenging experience no matter what our age. Age is not a barrier to achievement. As we grow older and learn more, we gain the confidence to take on new challenges.

Learn something new. Learn a musical instrument, a foreign language, flower arranging, calligraphy, typing, or computer programming. There are many stimulating new things waiting to be learned. If we fill our days with accomplishments and novelty, there will be no time for self-pity.

One of my learning projects has been the writing of this book. It has been, in itself, a healing experience. Committing to paper gossamer thoughts and obscure feelings has cleansed my memory. Years ago when I first began working out my grief frustrations by committing my feelings to paper, I did not know that my scribbles would eventually evolve into a book. Writing this book has been like talking with a caring friend, one who listens without interrupting, one who accepts me as I am.

The Healing Power
of Responsibility

Responsible living does not happen by accident. It must be cultivated, apprehended, and developed. We can blame the circumstances of our lives for our weaknesses, failures, and insecurities, but eventually we need to face the fact that we are our own worst enemies. We fear failure. We need to believe that we can make it. Responsibility, when cultivated, helps bring healing.

As we begin to believe in ourselves, we begin to see opportunities. But every opportunity involves a risk—a risk of making a wrong decision, a risk of failure. There are times when those decisions do not turn out right, but still we go on. We try again. Such is the principle of taking responsibility for ourselves.

• *Taking Responsibility for Yourself* •
There are things the widowed must learn to do: balance a checkbook, put gas in the car, make decisions, live by a budget. New things may seem overwhelming until we put

them in perspective and begin to learn by doing.

Never having put gas in my car before, I knew nothing of what to do first. But faced with the reality of either learning to do it or walking, I got out at the gas pump, read the instructions on the pump, and wham-o! I learned. And it was not the life-threatening event I had imagined it to be.

The same is true with balancing a checkbook, making decisions, and living by a budget. Most widows are faced with living on reduced income, and more than likely, bills will exceed income. Such was my situation.

I was faced with a decision. In any kind of decision making, a simple formula helps:

1. Identify the problem.
2. Determine the alternatives.
3. Compare the alternatives.
4. Select the most appropriate.

In my dilemma, I worked out my problem this way:

1. Identify the problem: My bills exceeded my income.
2. Determine the alternatives: I could either (a) sell my home and move to an apartment or (b) get a second job.
3. Compare the alternatives: (a) Selling my home would take time, and taking care of a small apartment would give me too much free time to mope; on the other hand, money from my equity would see me through my emergency. (b) Since I did not get off work from my regular job

until 5:00 PM, the second job would have to begin after that; a second job would keep my mind occupied with things other than grief; I would be tired enough to sleep at night; the money would see me through my present emergency.

4. Select the most appropriate: In my situation I selected (b) the second job.

I found a suitable second job, which proved to be a wise decision. It kept my mind occupied with thoughts other than grief.

Becoming responsible for new decisions can seem threatening and overwhelming. This formula, when applied to various problems, will bring scattered thoughts together. Jigsaw-puzzle pieces will find their proper place, and the picture of a new life will begin to emerge. Sometimes the solution may not work, but often it is less stressful to make a wrong decision than no decision at all. If one solution does not work, we must try another. The important thing is to try. Indecisiveness creates stressful situations. Taking responsibility for ourselves increases our feelings of self-esteem and self-worth.

For every difficult decision, we need an inner strength that will push us to confront the challenges and keep us going. Positive feelings help us overcome inertia and focus on the future. The greatest incentive is the desire to seize control of one's life.

• *Money Management* •

Money management is a part of our total life. It takes practice to become a smart and responsible consumer, someone who can balance a checkbook and avoid debt.

People who have difficulty in making both ends meet, can often benefit by using a budget. When we hear the word budget it usually conjures up in our mind a harsh, strict set of rules and, as a result, leaves a bad taste in our mouth. But a budget is nothing more than a plan to aid us in making the best possible use of our money. The word *budget* comes from the French word *bougette*, meaning a bag or wallet.

The first step in planning a budget is to set the goals you hope to achieve. If you want to take a vacation, you must include this goal in your budget planning. If, however, you have only ten dollars a month to set aside, taking a vacation may seem impossible. In order to plan for a vacation, you may have to spend less on other things and perhaps go without some things. But this is what setting goals means. From all the possible ways to spend your money, you select the things you want most. Then you spend and save accordingly. Your budget helps you reach your own goals.

A well-planned budget usually provides for three kinds of goals:

1. *Long-range goals,* such as home ownership, college education for children, retirement independence.

2. *Intermediate goals.* These cannot be attained immediately but can be reached in a few months or years, such as vacation trips, purchase of new automobile, or new furniture.

3. *Immediate goals.* These are needs that must be met every week or month, such as food, rent, utilities, clothing, church.

In addition, wise people save a little each week or month for emergencies. Emergencies could include such things as doctor bills or repair bills.

Once you have determined your goals, estimate your income. Then revise your expenditures (the amounts you plan to spend) so that they do not exceed your income. A budget is in balance when income equals expenditures plus savings. A balanced budget means that you are working toward your goals in a satisfactory fashion. A budget not in balance means that expenses exceed income, and some goals are losing out.

To make a budget work, keeping accurate records is important. Payment of bills by check helps to provide a permanent record. A spindle or file placed in a convenient spot is helpful for collecting cash register tapes. A small blank pad is useful in recording expenditures where there is no receipt.

Some people use an envelope system in carrying out their budget plans. They prepare envelopes marked "Food," "Rent," "Gas," "Church," "Vacation," and so on. Every payday they place the money allocated for each item in the appropriate envelope.

To summarize, here are the rules for making a budget work:

1. Determine goals on a sound and realistic basis.
2. Balance income with expenditures and savings.
3. Keep accurate records.
4. Compare actual expenditures and savings with the budget frequently and make adjustments when necessary.

Remember, a budget is only a plan and should be flexible. If you have children, sketch out to them a general idea of where your money must go on a regular basis. They need not know every detail of your budget, but how can they accept limitations unless they know where the limits come from? This will not only teach kids the many month-ly claims on your income but may help motivate them to be part of the solution to money problems.

When you show them by your budget that you do not have money for a certain thing, it will entice them to save from their own allowance for wanted things and perhaps encourage them to mow a lawn or babysit for needed funds. When you teach money management to your chil-dren, you instill in them the coping skills they will need to succeed in life.

It requires practice to understand how to use money wisely and what it takes to earn it. When we practice sound financial guidelines we are ready to face this tough, economic world on our own, thereby giving ourselves a precious gift: the key to self-sufficiency.

When we can regard changes in our lifestyle as chal-lenges instead of threats, we are well on the way to accept-ing responsibility for ourselves.

Accepting responsibility through grief has been a learn-ing experience. Change and growth were thrust upon me. Through it all, I found the greatest gift: I found myself.

• *Traditions We Treasure* •

During grief, Christmas is a time of sadness. While others get caught up in the rush of the season, those suffering from grief endure rather than enjoy the holidays. Holidays release memories of recent losses and ghosts of happier times.

To combat this sadness, the responsibility involved in carrying out traditions we treasure will see us through this season, bringing a calmness not otherwise felt. Through its traditions, Christmas connects people to others and to larger ideas and values, getting us outside ourselves by encompassing others.

Traditions hold families together. They give us a sense of stability, allowing us a way to express our love for one another. Love of holiday traditions sparks our imagination each year as we strive to bring to life the simplicity of bygone times. When decorating our homes, we are often drawn to objects reminiscent of an earlier era. Holiday memories wait until that time each year when we rediscover them, unpack our treasures, and are magically transported to a time and place waiting to be remembered. The spirit of Christmas Past comes romantically alive.

There is comfort and healing in familiar traditions we treasure. As we experience this healing through our own special family traditions, let us also include three traditions that God Himself instituted on that long-ago first Christmas.

1. *Responsibility to God.* In preparation for the drama that would unfold on that holy night in Bethlehem, God's search for the proper girl led him to a young Jewish maiden named Mary. No doubt, it was Mary's love for Jehovah along with her character that drew her to Him. The responsibility to bear, to rear, and to educate the Son of God was an awesome task. With the same hopes and dreams of other young maidens, Mary was an ordinary girl. The Almighty, however, gave her an extraordinary mission, altered the circumstances of her life, and called her for a deeper walk with Him.

Imagine the excitement Mary must have felt to know the Messiah would come through her. Yet she stood alone in her joy because others did not understand. They turned away, thinking she had brought shame on her family and on Joseph.

Sometimes God stops the ordinary course of our lives and alters it for greater trusts. But when He does, there is always a responsibility involved. Mary was true in her responsibility to God.

2. *Responsibility to Family.* Joseph likewise was an ordinary man, with the same hopes and dreams that young men have today. He had found the girl of his dreams and wanted to marry her. Eventually, children would come along, and they would rear a family. But God altered the predictable course of his life.

Imagine Joseph's confusion when he learned of Mary's condition. He had to decide whether to believe the angel of the Lord in the dream or to believe apparent circumstances. True, it was against nature for a virgin to conceive, yet Joseph chose to believe that Jehovah could alter nature. A noble man, he chose to accept the responsibility to protect and care for Mary and her child, taking them to himself as his family. The Bible says that he was a just man; even before the angel's explanation to him he was not willing to make Mary a public example. Unquestionably, Joseph was true in his responsibility to family.

3. *Responsibility to Others.* It was God Himself who chose to include all of heaven in the events of that hushed, silent night, for He sent the mighty heavenly host who appeared praising God: "Glory to God in the highest, and on earth peace, good will toward men."

God also chose nearby shepherds keeping watch over their flock that night to join in the joyous celebration. "Behold I bring you good tidings of great joy," proclaimed

God's messenger. "Unto you is born this day in the city of David, a Saviour, which is Christ the Lord."

Then they were ushered into the holy presence of the Christ child: "Ye shall find the babe wrapped in swaddling clothes, lying in a manger." God chose lowly shepherds to be among the first of humanity to touch deity.

Lastly, it was also God Himself who chose to include the whole world in the greatest story ever told by sending His star in the East to guide the steps of the wise men who brought gifts to the newborn King.

Our Christmas traditions should include not only responsibility to God and family but also responsibility to others: to the heavenly host (our church family), to the nearby shepherds (our friends and neighbors), and to the wise men who come from afar (our world as a whole).

The special joy of Christmas can transcend any other time of year, and the special traditions of Christmas can bring healing to a hurting heart and comfort to a grieving spirit.

The Healing Power of a Healthy Self-Image

U sually, self-esteem dies with a spouse. Becoming whole again requires a healthy self-image. When self-esteem is gone, how do we revive it?

True motivation and excitement come from within. We cannot fake them. Excitement about life and happiness with ourselves build character. Here is the basis of developing a healthy self-image.

• *What Is Self-Esteem?* •

Self-respect. To have self-esteem is to have self-respect. *Webster's Dictionary* aptly defines self-respect as "proper regard for the dignity of one's own character." To have self-respect, we must consider our own character as being worthy to be respected. A person with no self-respect is saying silently but oh so loudly to others that his character is not worthy to be respected. Others feel that we know ourselves better than anyone knows us. Therefore, if we have no respect for ourselves, others will not respect us. Respect demands respect.

The first step in learning to have respect for ourselves is learning to love God. When we realize the goodness and the greatness of our God we become confident that we can handle life; we can face troubles. In loving God, we learn to love ourselves, and when we learn to love ourselves, we never want to hurt others.

Having respect for ourselves is mirrored in our attitude toward God and our fellow man. We transfer to others the attitude we have toward ourselves. Loving ourselves, we wish good for others. If we are not happy with ourselves, we will not be happy with anybody else.

Pride. A certain type of pride is necessary for achieving a healthy self-image: pride in looking your best at all times, pride in a job well done, pride in accomplished goals. A widowed person sometimes loses this pride. Her special person is gone. She has no one for whom to look her best. But boosting our self-respect will once again reactivate this healthy type of pride. During grief, there is a certain stage where "nothing matters anymore." If self-esteem can be activated at this point, hopelessness will dissolve into purpose, drive, and motivation.

The type of pride I am talking about is not egotism, conceit, vanity, or haughtiness. To be conceited is to exalt oneself above others, to look down on the accomplishments of others. The Bible strongly warns against pride in this sense.

• *Understanding Yourself* •

What makes your personality the way it is? Have you ever adjusted your personality to fit the person you are with? By living this way you are portraying a mirror image of what others expect you to be. You mirror others' expectations and have no real expectations of yourself.

We often accept others' ideas of us without stopping to ask, "Am I really that way?" Peer pressure is prevalent no matter what our age. But there comes a time when we will have to stand alone. In order to have a healthy self-image, we must face peer pressure squarely; we must be ourselves and not a mirror image of what others expect us to be.

There was a certain time during widowhood when I felt pressured on all sides—pressured by colleagues at work, by friends, by family. I felt I was constantly being pressed to conform to others' expectations. Until, that is, I decided not to adjust my personality to suit others but decided instead to live by self-chosen principles. I chose to live by the principle "Because it is right," not on the basis of "What will she (or he) think?" or "Will I fit in if I do it (or don't do it)?"

Living by self-chosen principles revived my self-image, gave me a boost, and helped me to be real. A real person acts the way he really is. He is what he seems to be. A false person acts the way others expect him to act. A real person trusts himself, lives in the present, is not afraid to express his true emotions, dares to think for himself, and lives by his own convictions. Are you a real person?

• *Accepting Yourself* •

Everyone is different, with different looks and different talents. Most often we put the emphasis on what we do not have instead of what we do have.

What do you like about yourself? The color of your hair? Your eyes? Your musical ability? Learn to develop a liking for the things about you that you cannot change.

Learn to dwell on the good things about yourself, and the things you do not like will become microscopic instead of monumental. Learn to like the things you cannot change—height, bone structure, color of eyes, certain talents (or lack of them). God made you with these characteristics for a purpose. Learn to like what God likes. If you reject the way God made you, you will find it hard to place confidence in Him in the other areas of life.

Fear of rejection will often cause us to miss the fellowship with others that we need. Bashfulness and self-consciousness are the result of thinking about our weaknesses. We need to dwell on positive strengths rather than negative weaknesses.

Remembering some bad decision, we say, "I could kick myself for being so stupid." We look back on actions of yesterday with shame and remorse. We cannot forget and we refuse to forgive ourselves. This is a form of self-hatred.

"I just can't do anything right!" Have you ever said this after an embarrassing blunder? Have you ever heard someone say, "I hate myself!" These are dangerous signposts of self-rejection and self-hatred. Self-rejection will eventually blame God for the way He has created us.

Consequently, the basic step toward a healthy self-image is learning to accept ourselves by constructing new thought patterns that place a value and a purpose in the person we are.

Make a list of changes in yourself that you would like to make. Correct what you can. Then learn to live with the things you cannot change. Finally, learn to like the things you cannot change. Commit yourself to cooperate with God's plan of developing your inward character.

• *Sticks and Stones* •

The tongue can no man tame (James 3:8).

Set a watch, O LORD, before my mouth; keep the door of my lips (Psalm 141:3).

A healthy self-image is not complete without a Christ-controlled tongue.

I was watching a group of children at play one day when suddenly a small voice rang out, "Sticks and stones may break my bones, but words will never hurt me!" The tear-stained cheeks of the small boy dramatically contradicted his loud outburst. As I listened to this childish chant, my mind leaped automatically to an almost forgotten yester-year and the reminiscences of long-ago childhood days.

How grown-up we thought we were when we quoted that phrase, yet deep down in our childish hearts we knew that words do hurt. Idle words are the "sticks and stones" that scar the soul. They live deep in the subconscious and are not easy to overcome.

Jesus warned us in the Scriptures that on judgment day we will "give account" of "every idle word" (Matthew 12:36). What a sobering thought!

Webster's Dictionary defines *idle* as "without worth or basis; useless; vain; inappropriate." So many times the words we speak are indeed "without worth or basis; useless; vain; inappropriate." They are idle words.

The human tongue is physically small but, oh, what tremendous wreckage it can boast! The expression "I only open my mouth to change feet" is apt. Physical hurt fades, but hurt upon the inner man is sometimes carried to the grave. The scars of the "sticks and stones" of idle words are deeply embedded upon the soul of man.

Sticks and Stones of Tactlessness. Some people say what they think even if it hurts someone else. Their excuse is, "I'm just being honest." But if someone is hurt by our words, in reality, we are not being "honest" but are guilty of tactlessness and rudeness. To be tactful is an art and requires a love and concern for the feelings of others.

Sticks and Stones of Backbiting and Slander. The opposite is true with others. They are not tactless and rude. They would never say anything to hurt someone's feelings. Yet they will assassinate the character of another in his absence. This is backbiting and slander. Reputations are shattered through idle words. By pointing out a person's good qualities and forgetting the bad, we will never be guilty of shattering a reputation.

Sticks and Stones of Criticism. "Well, I only try to improve people," some would say. This is criticism and if not done with a tactful spirit can cause the alienation of the best of friends. To be critical is to impose one's own viewpoint on another. We should strive to see another's point of view.

Sticks and Stones of Flattery. "I like to be nice to people so I praise them," are the words of others. Praise is always nice to hear. Genuine praise is balm to the soul, but insincere praise is flattery. If we are guilty of the "sticks and stones" of flattery, let us look for our motives. Are we, perhaps, looking for flattery (praise) in return?

Sticks and Stones of Exaggeration and Lying. Are we hazy on some of the facts? Do we omit or add certain details, distorting the meaning so that our listener is deceived? Exaggeration can lead to lying.

Sticks and Stones of Breach of Confidence and Gossip. Something told to us in confidence should be forever locked within our heart, but unfortunately, some feel a sense of importance in passing along such information. This makes one guilty of a breach of confidence, and if it is repeated further becomes gossip. "Plain ole gossip," repeating something scandalous one has heard whether true or not, has wrecked more lives possibly than drugs or alcohol. Gossip scars the inner man.

The source of the words we speak is the heart. Jesus said, "Out of the abundance of the heart the mouth speaketh" (Matthew 12:34). What is in our heart eventually comes forth in our speech. "Keep thy heart with all diligence; for out of it are the issues of life" (Proverbs 4:23).

Have you ever been to the doctor and heard him say, "Stick out your tongue?" Why does he do that? Because by looking at your tongue he can tell the condition of your body. Likewise, we reveal the condition of our heart by our tongue. As we converse with a person, sooner or later he will reveal his true self through his speech.

There is something wrong with the fountain within if out of it flows both "blessing and cursing" (James 3:9-12). If one can praise God with one breath and talk against his fellow man with the next, something is drastically wrong at the source (the heart).

Our ability to communicate through speech is one of God's greatest gifts. But like so many other things that are a part of life, this great gift of speech can easily be misused.

Lord, help me not be guilty of the sticks and stones of idle words. "Let the words of my mouth, and the meditation of my heart, be acceptable in thy sight" (Psalm 19:14).

Marceal Clark
Hearing the music again!

Wedding Picture
Marceal Camp and Keith W. Clark, Sr. were married
October 26, 1991, in Longview, TX, at Calvary Christian Tabernacle.

The Healing Power
of Remarriage

Someone touched me on the shoulder. "Would you step outside so I can talk with you?"

Startled, I whirled around from the church bulletin board that I was reading.

It was Keith Clark, my friend Patti's father.

I had known Patti and her family ever since they moved to our city many years ago. Patti and I had been involved together in many church-related activities: teaching Sunday school and youth classes, writing plays and skits, being counselors and teachers at youth retreats, going on trips to conventions and conferences. My heart was saddened when Patti's sister died and then within a short period also her mother. Now her dad wanted to talk to me.

We stepped outside the door of the church away from the crowd. "Would you consider having coffee with me some night after church?" he asked.

I must have scared him when I said yes because he jumped in his truck and drove away. I assumed he meant to have coffee then, since it was after church. But, he told me later, no way could he do two things at once! He could not ask me out and then go—he was too rattled.

That was the beginning of our three-month courtship.

During those three months, this sensitive man taught me how to laugh again, an emotion I thought was dead forever.

We became "road runners" during those three months. We tried all the restaurants in town, went to all our church activities, went for coffee after Sunday night services (he finally got the nerve). We even went uninvited to a wedding rehearsal at a church in Gilmer, thinking that a revival meeting was going on. Red-faced, humiliated, we sneaked out when the pastor asked whether we were the parents of the bride or of the groom.

Marry again?

Yes, I've thought of it.

Marry you?

Yes, I'll marry you.

* * * * *

Years ago, when I first began thinking about writing this book and began writing down certain thoughts that were rattling around in my head, never in a thousand years did I think that I could be writing the final chapter about the healing power of remarriage. I had another ending in mind— a positive note but not quite that positive!

But the God I serve, the God who has been with me through every joy and hurt of life, saw this final chapter long before I did. I see his handiwork in every chapter of my life, every change point, every milestone, every ripple, every slightest breeze. He has been there through it all.

Keith W. Clark, Sr. and I were married October 26, 1991, in Longview, Texas, at Calvary Christian Tabernacle.

Keith is a sensitive man, well-acquainted with grief. Not only did he lose his wife of forty-six years but also a beautiful thirty-eight-year-old daughter.

Together, Keith and I have three sons, four daughters (one of whom is deceased), their spouses, sixteen grandchildren, and three dogs. Our hearts are full.

I read somewhere that love is to the human heart what flowers are to the hillside. Flowers cover naked, ragged places; grow around rocks and roots; cover wounds in the earth's surface; cover clay and bleak soil with beauty. So love covers ragged, rough spots in the human heart. The ragged, rough spots of my heart are forever covered by the beauty of Keith's love.

Here is why I titled this chapter "The Healing Power of Remarriage":

First, there is understanding. It's the way Keith quietly listens without interrupting when I feel the need to talk about my former hurts. It's the way I put my arms around him when he chokes up while talking about Linda, his daughter who died in the prime of life, or Nadine, his first wife, who suffered so much during her last days. It's the way we both understand that there is a part of each other we can never enter.

It's the way he's blind and deaf to my faults and weaknesses; it's when he goes to the woods with the three dogs and I understand his need to be alone. It's the way there is no need for words between us. We understand the other by just being together. Yet it's the way we can freely talk and share our innermost feelings. We are each other's best friend.

It's the way Keith says at nightfall, "I'll be back later," that I know he's going to the old iron gate to pray. There in the undisturbed wilds of nature where faraway civilization dares not intrude, chaperoned by distant stars and shimmering moon, he communes with God. The old iron gate has heard many secrets, many agonizing questions, many fears, many thanksgivings. That rusty iron gate is his refuge, his hideaway, his sanctuary, where he dwells "in the secret place of the Most High."

There is caring. It's when he gets an appeal for help and is quick to respond: to crippled children, to survivors of slain police officers, to flood victims. And then when there is no appeal, he is equally sensitive to the need and quick to respond: to missionaries, to evangelists, to the home church, to God's work. It's giving boxes of food anonymously to the needy and putting sacks of his freshly-picked garden vegetables on the hood of every car at prayer meeting.

It's planting dozens of rosebushes when he learns the rose is my favorite flower. It's putting on his "nurse suit" and tenderly caring for me when I'm sick, making sure I take my medication and cooking my meals.

It's scattering hundreds of pounds of birdseed in the wintertime so the wild birds won't starve; burying sweet potatoes in the field so the deer will have food through the cold, icy months; scattering nuts for the squirrels and dried corn for the rabbits. It's cooking chicken for Prissy, Missy, and Skippy, the three dogs, so they will have a hot meal.

In the summertime, it's making sure the hummingbird feeders are kept clean and full of fresh, sugared water; making scrambled-egg sandwiches for the dogs; cleaning out the bluebird houses in preparation for the first bluebirds, then crying when the mother bluebird is killed and her eggs abandoned. It's watching a tiny wren build a nest on our front porch and then rejoicing when she teaches her young to fly. It's his respect for life that causes him to merely watch instead of act as baby wolves frolic and play along the fence row.

There is sharing. It's Keith plunging his hands in hot dish water and washing the dishes, and then when I protest, turning a willfully deaf ear. When I try to help save our garden during a drought by dragging water hoses hundreds of feet, he's grateful. And then, when I try to help harvest our blackberry crop and get my hair tangled up in the vines and briars and can't get loose, he laughs.

It's getting up at 5:00 AM and together taking our produce to the farmers' market. It's setting up an assembly line in the kitchen when we make pickles. It's crying together when doctors in recent months confirmed that Keith had cancer. It's rejoicing together when surgery succeeded in removing all the cancer. It's kneeling together in prayer.

There is fun. Last evening in the chilling night air, we romped in the woods with Prissy, Missy, and Skippy, then collapsed in each other's arms from laughing at their silly antics.

We get hysterical remembering all the many times we've wandered around lost when taking trips. We enjoy going to different church conferences but have learned to start early. In Oklahoma City, we spent three hours trying to locate the church; in Corpus Christi, four hours; in Austin, two; in Jackson, three. And, then, in Marshall (twenty miles from home) we never found it.

We laugh remembering the way Keith proposed. "Be sure to take her to an expensive restaurant and ask her by candlelight," was his daughter-in-law's advice. He took me to Shoney's underneath a glaring, naked, two-hundred-watt light bulb.

There are surprises. It's bringing me red roses for no special reason. It's coming home and saying, "Baby, get your duds together, we're going away for the weekend."

On his birthday, I left him little post-it notes saying "I love you" stuck on the bathroom mirror, in the refrigerator, in his underwear drawer, in his shoes, in his shirts, in the pocket of a coat, stuffed in his favorite coffee cup, and even stuck to the dog-food sack. When Keith realized they were everywhere, he tore the house apart until he found them all. Then, the next day with his penciled postscript of "Me, too!," I discovered the same notes in my lingerie drawer, my purse, on the mirror, the coffeepot, the stove, my closet, my pillow.

Then, there is knowing. I know Keith will have four dozen eggs in the refrigerator at all times. ("They were on sale and, besides, the dogs like scrambled-egg sandwiches.") I know he will hide the last piece of coconut pie and buy a sack of candy when he goes to town. I know he will get us lost every time we go somewhere.

Keith knows I will leave every light on in the house. He knows I will cook enough for "fifty people," mess up every dish in the kitchen, and lose the keys to the truck on a regular basis. He knows that I will also get us lost every time we go somewhere.

Finally, there is faith. Keith and I help each other to acknowledge the cycles of life and to realize that the joys far outweigh the sorrows. Faith keeps us going, gives us a sense of stability, and allows us a way to express our love for one another. Faith is a feeling of the heart stimulated by two caring people who help one another hear the music again.

• *The Story of Missy: Lessons from a Mongrel Dog* •

The rain had stopped and the weather had changed. A chill had come up, and a wind was rising. I could hear the sighing of the trees and the whistling of the wind as it rounded the corner of the house and bounced against the windows.

Where was she?

My nose pressed against the windowpane as I peered into the eerie blackness of the night. My husband, Keith, had given up the search for her. Missy, our little doe-eyed mongrel dog, had been missing for three days now, but somehow I couldn't get her off my mind, for she had become so much a part of my new life. She had accepted me so unreservedly as a part of her life that I felt a tremendous sense of loss at her disappearance.

"Baby, out here in the country it's not uncommon for the wolves to get the little dogs. I've already lost two to them." My husband's words were not reassuring. He at sixty-seven and I at sixty-one had been married less than two months. A widow and a widower were experiencing the joy of a new-found love.

Tears trickled down my face as I thought with gratitude of my new life. Our pastor, during the marriage ceremony, encouraged us to enter our new phase of life with confidence and with joy, not forgetting the past but letting go of the past. There is a difference. Only as we let go of what once was can we go on to what can be.

With the hope and joy of a new bride I had moved into Keith's country home situated on sixty-one acres of land nestled in the piney woods of East Texas on the banks of Little Cypress Bayou. With the exuberance of newlyweds, we had romped with the three dogs—Prissy (the aristocrat),

Missy (the mongrel), and Skippy (the clown)—who had welcomed me wholeheartedly into their world.

Now, pressing my face against the windowpane and staring into the night, I remembered those long, exhilarating walks deep into the piney woods in the chilling night air as the dogs happily flushed out raccoons and rabbits.

Oh, Missy, where are you?

The wind gained in force while rain once again lashed the windows. There was a shrilling crescendo of wind and a clatter, and I could feel chill air breathing down my neck. I rushed to close the door that had blown open and bolted it against the onslaught of the storm.

The electric power had long since gone off—something this city girl was not used to, but which I soon learned was common in country life. The flickering light of the oil lamps cast an unreal and otherworldly glow, shadowy forms making fleeting impressions. As we prepared for bed, the dim halo of light seemed to accentuate the fierceness of the storm. I slept fitfully as the rain slashed in sheets.

It was the next morning that we found Missy. Exploring the rainswept piney woods in the aftermath of the storm, Keith stumbled upon her still, contorted form a few hundred yards from our back door.

"Baby, she's been shot," he shouted, and I could hear his urgent voice echoing through the dripping trees.

Keith gingerly wrapped Missy in a blanket, bundled her on the front seat of the pickup truck, and then started the long ride into town to the West Loop Animal Hospital. There Dr. Balliett gave her an anesthetic and began the tedious job of trying to save her shattered leg.

"Three days she was missing, huh? Mr. Clark, looks like those deer hunters in your back woods mistook Missy for a deer." The doctor was gently feeling all her bones. "Missy's got spunk," Dr. Balliett continued. "She's in so much pain but nevertheless determined to drag herself home. She'll have to stay here with us for a few days. This leg has been nearly shot off—may lose it yet—and I'll have to watch her closely."

Coming home after a few days' stay with Dr. Balliett at the animal hospital, Missy reveled in being the center of attention. Sporting her newly splinted leg, complete with the wicked-looking pins that stuck out on both sides, she enjoyed Keith's extra attention as he made her the special scrambled-egg sandwiches she adored (with mayonnaise— Skippy liked mustard while Prissy preferred pimento cheese). I laughingly told Keith that with all the attention he lavished on his dogs they would be heartbroken if they ever discovered they're mere dogs and not his children.

I watched Missy over the next months as she adjusted to her new life. Almost a tangible thing, her love of life was a joy to behold. Her handicap didn't stop her from romps with Keith and me and Prissy and Skippy. Racing to the mailbox at the end of the lane, she learned to run faster with three legs than Prissy and Skippy could with their four, outdistancing them every time, much to their embarrassment.

I watched as she went running through the woods on the trail of an elusive rabbit or squirrel, her splint and pins dragging up all kinds of underbrush, pine needles, and pine cones. "Come here, Missy," Keith would laugh when she looked at him so pleadingly. "Let's get you untangled so you can get on with the chase."

Her handicap didn't stop her from joining in the fun as Keith and I scrambled for the front porch swing. We were never quite fast enough to have it to ourselves. It was always a family affair with three dogs grinning like Cheshire cats as they plopped down contentedly in our laps.

I watched Missy lead the scampers of the five of us through the fence and down the hill to the river. Three dogs, like children, bailed off the bank for a quick swim, and then Missy, when a fish nibbled at her foot, flew out of the water as if she were being chased by an alligator!

One day, in her exuberance of life, Missy fell while climbing over the fence. Dr. Balliett's X-rays showed the bone had been refractured when the pins got tangled up in the wire fence. With new splint and new pins, Missy started the slow process of healing all over again. Even so, she never laid around and expected to be pampered. Getting on with her life—her new life—was Missy's main objective.

Through the months, I watched as she, gingerly at first, started putting her weight on her injured foot. Today, ten months have passed since Missy was shot. She's ecstatic now that the cumbersome splint and pins are finally gone for good. Her leg is crooked. She has a bad limp. She practically never puts her full weight on her crippled leg, preferring to run on her three good legs, but still outdistancing Prissy and Skippy. Regardless of all this, her exuberance and love of life seem to increase day by day.

Watching Missy adjust to her new life has caused me to remember how much of my own healing over the widowhood years came from involving myself totally outside my old life. I learned, though it took a few years, that pain is a natural part of living. Just as surely as the Resurrection followed the suffering of the Cross, so the joys of life come only to those who walk faithfully through its pains.

I learned, though it took a few more years, that when

we release our grasp on our desires, we are at last open to receive what God desires for us. When I let go of my demands for how I thought my world should be, I found I had strengths I was unaware of—just like Missy. With widowhood came the surfacing of an inner self I had never explored before—just like Missy.

I can't help thinking that no matter how much joy that old life gave, it is the flow and thrust of the new that gives us today and makes us the way we are.

Keith Clark with Prissy, Missy, and Skippy.

143

Keith and son, Keith W. Clark, Jr., pastor of Austin Tabernacle, Austin, Texas.

The Clark Family— Keith's first wife, Nadine (seated) and daughter, Linda Jo (back row, far right) are both deceased.